WE THY GLORY SING

Snapshots & Remembrances from the History of Columbia College, 1854–2016

Ed Eubanks Creative Services
195 Mack Edwards Drive
Oakland, TN 38060
www.eubankscreative.com

Ordering Information:
Quantity sales. Special discounts are available on quantity purchases by corporations, associations, bookstores, wholesalers, and others. For details, contact the designer at the address above.

Edited & designed by Ed Eubanks Creative Services. Printed in the United States of America

This book is printed using 50lb. 444 ppi archival paper that is produced according to Sustainable Forestry Initiative® (SFI®) Certified Sourcing.

We Thy Glory Sing! Snapshots & Remembrances from the History of Columbia College, 1854–2016
ISBN: 978-1-937063-03-0

13 14 15 16 17 18 19 20   10 9 8 7 6 5 4 3 2 1

EDITOR'S PREFACE

This book is the fruit of the work of many, who have turned a labor of love into a tribute to the institution they all adore. It is the product of more than a decade's worth of research, discussion, planning, and writing. Over that time, clippings from newspapers, newsletters, Methodist Conference proceedings, books, magazines, letters, and personal accounts were compiled into a collection totaling more than 500 pages worth of material, along with dozens of photos accompanying these clippings.

Throughout the editing process, it was clear that Belinda Gergel (class of 1972) and Elizabeth "Tootsie" DuRant (class of 1950) wrote or edited portions of many clippings, clarifying and/or unifying them into more presentable segments. Likewise, the fingerprints of Edith Hause (class of 1956), Janet Cotter (class of 1956), Judy Cannon (class of 1974), MaryAnn Smith Eubanks Crews (class of 1959), Ann Harrell (class of 1957), Lisa Livingston (class of 1991), Carla Moore (class of 1994), and Becky Swanson (class of 1957) are all over these pages. The book before you is *their* work. Their names may not appear in the footnotes, but the credit is theirs as much as those who happen to receive attribution.

So much content that deserved inclusion in this work nevertheless had to be cut; many people, departments, traditions, and events that would fill the pages of a fuller history and swell the hearts of its readers are, sadly, not in this volume. Readers may regret that their own experiences from CC are not adequately reflected because of this, but I hope not—rather, I join the committee in the hope that the book before you will at least touch on the very best of the college, and of her storied and magnificent history. And, too, the hope that those gems that were omitted may one day find their way into a more comprehensive collection.

It was my privilege to come alongside this team of sisters for the very last stages of the project, and my work (which was, essentially, to reduce their copious collection into a publishable form) has been minimal compared to theirs. I am sure I speak for the student body, the faculty and staff, the alumnae, and all in Columbia and South

Carolina (and beyond) who appreciate the importance of Columbia College when I say: thank you, faithful ladies, for your tireless effort and labor to see this volume to its completion.

The following remembrance from Professor Michael Broome, one of many that had to be amended significantly for the final manuscript but which, like the rest, told a story of the community that Columbia College truly is, was striking in how it embodied the spirit and tenacity that led to the book:

> My office in the Department of English isn't far from the downstairs room in Edens Library where our college archives are stored. I've popped in occasionally to watch the work on the book wherein my rambling reflection will reside. Gathered around a large work table have been Edith Hause, Elizabeth DuRant, Janet Cotter, Judy Cannon, MaryAnn Crews, Ann Harrell, and Belinda Gergel. Archival material—books, organizational minutes, old photos, laminated newspaper articles, much more—is stacked around them, over them, beyond them.
>
> They've worked diligently on this book. They appear to love their work—and their time together. They're what Columbia College is all about.

I cannot help but agree: the book you hold in your hands is a demonstration of what Columbia College has brought to our world: strong, well-educated women whose work is meaningful, whose devotion to others is precious, and above all, whose love for the college is unquestionable.

CONTENTS

INTRODUCTION

On behalf of the History Committee of the Sesquicentennial Committee, I am pleased to introduce to you *We Thy Glory Sing: Snapshots from the History of Columbia College, 1854–2016*. In January of 2004, Janet Cotter, co-chair with Ginger Crocker of the Sesquicentennial Celebration, asked Elizabeth "Tootsie" DuRant, Becky Swanson, Anne Harrell and me to serve as a History Committee to look at ways we could preserve the college's 150-year history. Shortly afterward I became chairman of this committee.

After one meeting, we realized we needed Dr. Belinda Gergel and Edith Hause to join our committee. They agreed and everyone began working hard on gathering historical data. Tootsie, Becky and Belinda visited the archives weekly and pulled interesting newspaper articles, magazine articles, and articles from other books written about Columbia College. Edith, Anne and MaryAnn worked on getting the alumnae association information. Belinda wrote the introductions and organized the articles for each of the six chapters. Judy Cannon and Lisa Livingston started meeting with us. Later Rita Livingston, Nancy Bunch, Helen Grant, Margie Mitchell and Sara Snell joined our committee. Marley Lybrand, then a recent graduate in my office, typed all of the articles for Chapters 1–4 and some of Chapter 5 into electronic documents. Rebecca Munnerlyn became our consultant and liaison on finding a printer and getting the book ready for print. For the last year, a smaller group made of Belinda, Janet, Edith, Tootsie, Judy and I worked almost weekly on finding the pictures for all chapters and finishing the longest and most recent chapter 5. Numerous words of thanks are due to all of these

people for all of their hard work on this project.

The book is a compilation of documents, articles, pictures, and other collections showing the history of the college, beginning with the denomination's announcement at Washington Street Methodist Church of the founding of a women's college up to the present. It is a compelling story of a college that has endured many hardships over its 150-year history. But as President Emeritus R. Wright Spears so beautifully stated on the night of the 1964 fire, "Nothing has been destroyed this night that cannot be rebuilt." It is a book about people who love Columbia College and who believe that "she who has been shall ever be, wise, good and true eternally."

The committee asked for sponsors of the book, and thanks to all of those listed who responded to the call, the book was fully funded. Money from the sale of books will go back to the college to be used for the Alumnae Scholarship Fund.

We hope that you will read with joy and pride the story of our college. We hope that it will stir memories of a happy time in your life. We hope that it will make alumnae and other friends of the college proud to have been a part of this great place. We hope that it will make you "sing the praise of her we love."

MaryAnn Smith Eubanks Crews
Class of 1959
Chair of History Book Committee

Committee members—front row, left to right: Janet Alexander Cotter, MaryAnn Smith Eubanks Crews, Elizabeth "Tootsie" DuRant. Back row, left to right: Judy Jones Cannon, Belinda Friedman Gergel, Lisa Kennerly Livingston, Edith Collins Hause, Anne Turner Harrell. Absent: Becky Glover Swanson, Sara Snell and Rebecca Munnerlyn. Others who assisted in the early stages were Rita Williams Livingston, Nancy Burch Bunch, Helen Nelson Grant, Margie Mitchell and Marley Lybrand Douglas.

Part I:
Early History

CHAPTER 1—THE BEGINNING

Prior to 1850, only one school was owned and controlled by the South Carolina Conference of the Methodist Episcopal Church, South: the Cokesbury Conference School in the town of Cokesbury, SC, which opened in 1836. The Methodist Church had been a pioneer in denominational education in the South; the Georgia Conference had Wesleyan Female College (said to be the oldest college for women in America), Emory College, and other short-lived minor schools. Centenary Institute, LaGrange College, Oak Bowery Female College and Macon Female Collegiate Institute belonged to the Alabama Conference. In Louisiana, Centenary College had been established for twenty-five years. Also present were Emory and Henry College in Virginia and the Asheville Female College in North Carolina.

By the early 1850s, a number of South Carolina Methodists had become advocates for higher education. In addition to supporting the Cokesbury School, their efforts also resulted in the chartering of Wofford College in Spartanburg for men and the Carolina Female Institute for women in Anson County, North Carolina. Yet, the need for a centrally-located school was soon evident. In 1853 the South Carolina Methodist Conference, held in Sumterville, ordered that an exploratory committee should meet at the earliest possible time, composed of delegates from all localities applying for a school to be established, and of five representatives from its own body. This committee would determine the number and locations of the colleges, and the measures necessary for their immediate establishment.

The following places were represented in the committee: Columbia, Camden, Newberry, Laurens, Union, Williamston, Bascomville, and Spartanburg. Deliberations were full, spirited and courteous, extending through a morning and afternoon session, and ending in the selection, at the first ballot, of Columbia and Spartanburg as the cities for locating two female colleges under the control and patronage of the Conference. Those appointed to a building committee for the Columbia Female College included: A. Wallace, W.W. Walker, S.S. McCully, T.H. Wade, and R. Bryce. For the

Spartanburg College, Messrs. S. Bobo, J.W. Tucker, J.B. Tolleson, TOP Vernon, and D.W. Moore. They were instructed to proceed immediately to make arrangements for putting up a suitable building, so that the institution may be staffed and their halls opened for instruction at an early period in the next year.

Columbia Female College was founded in 1854 at Washington Street Methodist Church pictured c.1875. Photograph courtesy of Washington Street United Methodist Church Archives.

The minutes of Conference report:

> At the instance of public-spirited gentlemen who are deeply interested in this subject a committee was raised at the late meeting of Conference to take the matter in hand and receive proposals from suitable localities for the erection of a college for young ladies. Such institutions abound and prosper in our Sister Conference beyond the Savannah River and there is no reason to delay much longer an enterprise so generally deemed important by the Methodist public opinion of this state.

Thus, the following was adopted:

> 'Resolved, that a committee of five be appointed to receive any offers that that may be made on the subject of establishing a Female College in some central or suitable position in this state; and if they shall deem it necessary to act in the recess of the Conference they are hereby clothed with power to do so as Commissioners in behalf of the South Carolina Conference.'

Trustees for the new Columbia Female College were selected at the 1854 Annual Conference, and by December of that year a charter was granted by the South Carolina General Assembly. That charter read as follows:

"Be it enacted by the Senate and House of Representatives now met and sitting in General Assembly, and by the authority of the same, that Andrew Wallace, James S. Guignard, John Bryce, Robert Bryce, W.W. Walker, Thomas H. Wade, S.S. McCully, Dr. Alexander N. Talley, Dr. John W. Parker, Dr. John H. Boatwright, William Glaze, John Veal, W.B. Johnston, Dr. Whitefoord Smith, Nicholas Talley, William Martin, William Crook, William H. Flemming, Hilliard C. Parsons, John T. Wightman, Colin Murchison, John A. Porter, Claudius H. Pritchard, Dr. Jos. Cross, Samuel Leard, and Dr. Robert J. Boyd, and their successors in office, be, and they are hereby, created and constituted a body politic and corporate, by the name and style of "The Trustees of the Columbia Female College," for the

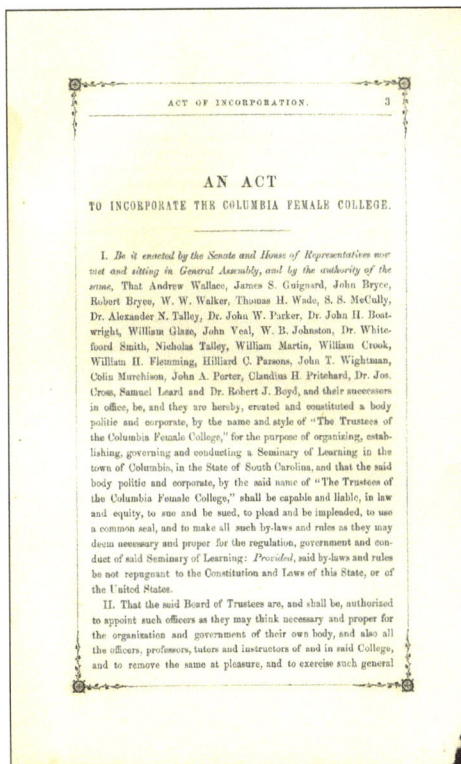

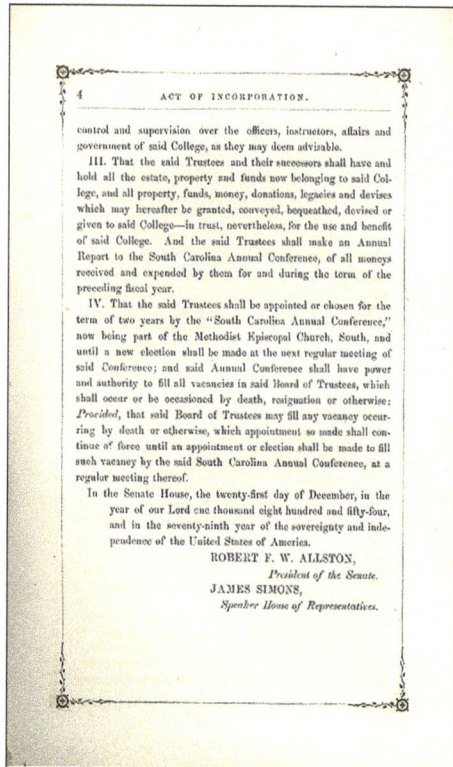

purpose of organizing, establishing, governing and conducting a Seminary of Learning in the town of Columbia, in the state of South Carolina, and that the said body politic and corporate, by the said name of "The Trustees of the Columbia Female College," shall be capable and liable, in law and equity, to sue and be sued, to plead and be impleaded, to use a common seal, and to make all such by-laws and rules as they may deem necessary and proper for the regulation, government and conduct of said Seminary of Learning: Provided, said by-laws and rules be not repugnant to the Constitution of Laws of this State, or of the United States.

That the said Board of Trustees are, and shall be, authorized to appoint such officers as they may think necessary and proper for the organization and government of their own body, and also all the officers, professors, tutors and instructors of and in said college, and to remove the same at pleasure, and to exercise such general control and supervision over the officers, instructors, affairs and government of said college, as they may deem advisable.

That the said Trustees and their successors shall have and hold all the estate, property and funds now belonging to said college, and all property, funds, money, donations, legacies and devises which may hereafter be granted, conveyed, bequeathed, devised or given to said college—in trust, nevertheless, for the use and benefit of said college. And the said Trustees shall make an Annual Report to the South Carolina Annual Conference, of all moneys received and expended by them for and during the term of the preceding fiscal year.

That the said Trustees shall be appointed or chosen for the term of two years by the "South Carolina Annual Conference," now being part of the Methodist Episcopal Church, South, and until a new election shall be made at the next regular meeting of said Conference; and said Annual Conference shall have power and authority to fill all vacancies in said Board of Trustees, which shall occur or be occasioned by death, resignation or otherwise: Provided, that said Board of Trustees may fill any vacancy occurring by death or otherwise, which appointment so made shall continue of force until an appointment or election shall be made to fill such vacancy by the said South Carolina Annual

Conference, at a regular meeting thereof.

In the Senate House, the twenty-first day of December, in the year of our Lord one thousand eight hundred and fifty-four, and in the seventy-ninth year of the sovereignty and independence of the United States of America."

Robert F.W. Allston,

President of the Senate.

James Simons,

Speaker House Of Representatives.

FIRST APPOINTMENTS AND EARLY FOUNDATIONS

Soon afterward, a lot was purchased on Plain Street (now Hampton Street) for $5,000, and the trustees hired G.E. Walker to draw architectural plans for the new structure. Work progressed, and the college cornerstone was dedicated in July 1856. Arrangements were made to commence building on January 1, 1856, but the work was not begun until April. In September, funds were exhausted and the contractor suspended operations. The 1857 Conference appointed Rev. William Martin as (financial) agent, who continued to serve in this position until 1860.

Trustees appointed Rev. Whitefoord Smith as the college's first president, and a faculty of six men and ten women welcomed the new college's first class in October 1859. Four months later, President Smith resigned and Rev. William Martin was appointed president.

Rev. Whitefoord Smith served as Columbia Female College's first president in 1854.

The buildings were completed and the college opened October 5, 1859, with Rev. Whitefoord Smith, D.D., as president, and Rev. T.E. Wannamaker, Mr. E. D'Ovilliers, Miss M. Dibble, and Miss M.C. Pelot as professors; W.H. Orchard and John Mayer in the Music department; J.B. Black, steward; and Mrs. Black, matron. The property, real and personal, cost $48,000. The tuition amounted to $47,135, of which $29,828 had been collected. Of the uncollected tuition, $14,406 was considered good, and indebtedness was $3,765.

The Reverend William Martin served as the second president of the college from 1860–62.

Among the outstanding philanthropists of the Methodist denomination was the widow Catherine

(Spencer) Verdier of St. Bartholomew's Parish, who owned six plantations and nearly 400 slaves in 1860. Her husband, Simon Verdier, who had come from France about 1800, operated a store for the planters who vacationed in Walterboro for the summers. Verdier himself became a planter, and also served his parish as state legislator and senator. When he died on June 21, 1853, he willed to his "beloved wife… all my real and personal estate" (they had no children).

Ten thousand dollars of this fortune was given to the new Methodist Female College at Columbia the year after Simon Verdier's death. Catherine Verdier, for many years and up to the time of her death, professed her saving faith in Jesus Christ; she was a constant and devout attendant on the ordinances of the gospel, a lover of the doctrine of grace, and ardently attached to the branch of Christ's church to which she belonged. In her philanthropic efforts, she demonstrated the greatest liberality toward all Christian denominations, including the Methodist church and its efforts for education.

In June 1860, 13 young women earned degrees, and commencement was held at Washington Street Church. A new era had begun in women's higher education in the South. Columbia College was born![1]

Columbia Female College on Plain Street (now Hampton Street).

---

1   Sources for this chapter: Southern Christian Advocate, February 17, 1854; Evelyn Barksdale Winn, "A History of Columbia College," master's thesis, University of South Carolina, 1927, pp. 3–6; Chalmers Gaston Davidson, *The Last Foray: The South Carolina Planters of 1860* (Columbia: Published for the South Carolina Tricentennial Commission by the University of South Carolina Press, 1971), pp. 101–102; John O. Wilson, *The History of Methodism*, pp. 21–22; *Catalogue of Columbia Female College*, 1860.

Addendum: Bylaws of the Columbia Female College

Government of the College

ART 1. The government of the college has been vested by an Act of Incorporation in a body known and styled as the "TRUSTEES OF THE COLUMBIA FEMALE COLLEGE." This Board of Trustees consists of twenty-six members, who, in accordance with the provisions of the Charter, are appointed biennially by the South Carolina Conference.

ART 2. The Board shall have charge of all the funds and property belonging to the college; shall receive all bequests and donations for its benefit, and shall elect all officers whose election is not otherwise herein provided for.

ART 3. The Board is empowered to fill all vacancies in its body occasioned by the death or resignation of its members.

ART 4. Seven members shall constitute a quorum for the transaction of all business connected with the college.

ART 5. The officers of the Board shall consist of a President, Secretary, and Treasurer, who shall be chosen by ballot, to serve for two years.

ART 6. During the deliberations of the Board, all motions, resolutions and propositions shall be submitted in writing, if required—the business of the Board being conducted in accordance with Parliamentary usage.

ART 7. There shall be one stated annual meeting of the Board, which shall take place on the last Wednesday in June.

ART 8. Occasional meetings shall be had at a time when demanded by the interests of the college, provided the call for such meetings shall proceed from the President of the Board, or from the President of the college and two members of the Board.

The Officers.

ART 1. The officers of the college should consist of a President, Professors, Teachers, Steward, and Matron, who shall be chosen by the Board, and hold their offices during its pleasure.

ART 2. No officer should resign his or her office without the consent of the Board, except upon six months' previous notice.

ART 3. The President, Professors and other officers shall reside in the college buildings, except by consent of the Board of Trustees to so otherwise.

The Faculty.

ART 1. The Faculty shall consist of the President and the male Professors.

ART 2. They shall have the immediate care and control of the pupils, and it shall be their duty not only to cultivate the minds, but also to have a scrupulous regard for the improvement in manners and morals of those committed to their care. They are empowered to frame all regulations which they may deem proper for the government and guidance of the students, provided that such regulations shall not conflict with laws established by the Board.

ART 3. There shall be the selection of text-books, in which, as in all things connected with the college, they shall be subject to the control of the Board.

ART 4. The jurisdiction of the Faculty shall extend to all matters pertaining to the internal administration of the college. It shall be their duty to preserve order and decorum among the students, and to interdict at all times promiscuous visits from persons unconnected with the college.

ART 5. There shall be weekly meetings of the Faculty for receiving reports of Teachers and Instructors; for noting the progress of the pupils, awarding censures and reproofs, and devising plans for the more effectual carrying out the college laws,—such deliberations being at all times secret, and differences of opinion among the Faculty studiously concealed from the knowledge of the pupils.

ART 6. The hours of study, recitation, recreation and meals shall be determined by the Faculty.

THE PRESIDENT.

ART 1. The President, as the chief executive of the college, shall exercise a general supervision of its affairs, enforce its laws and regulations, and adopt all measures consistent therewith for the maintenance of proper order and discipline among the students. He shall assure himself from time to time of the progress of the pupils in their several departments, and make any suggestions or arrangements which he may deem conducive to their more rapid advancement. He shall preside at all meetings of the Faculty, and when they are equally divided, shall have the casting vote. He shall award honors and degrees, and pronounce sentences, censures and reproofs.

ART 2. The President shall keep a book, in which the full name of every pupil, her parent or guardian, together with her post office and the date of her admission, shall be accurately entered.

ART 3. He shall receive all moneys paid for the tuition of pupils, and shall deposit them weekly in the hands of the college Treasurer.

ART 4. He shall make, or cause to be made, to every parent or guardian, a monthly report of the standing and conduct of pupils.

ART 5. He shall see that the rooms of the pupils are visited every night, after the last bell, by one of the female Teachers, who in turn shall perform this duty.

ART 6. In case of sickness or absence of the President, his office shall devolve upon one of the Professors, to be chosen by the Executive Committee, and the Professor so appointed shall, during such sickness or absence, discharge the executive functions of the President until relieved by the Board.

ART 7. The Professors and Teachers shall give instructions in several departments committed to them by the Board; they shall aid the President in enforcing order, and shall maintain a constant supervision of the conduct of the pupils, as well in the college grounds as elsewhere in the city of Columbia. It shall be their duty to see that the hours of study and retirement are observed, and report all delinquencies and offences at the weekly meetings of the Faculty.

THE PUPILS.

ART 1. No resident pupil shall receive instructions in any ART, science or polite accomplishment, without the consent of the President.

ART 2. No student shall be at liberty to leave the chapel or recitation room during their exercises, except by permission of one of the faculty or teachers.

ART 3. Each resident pupil shall be required to attend Divine service, with one or more of the Faculty or resident Teachers, every Sabbath, in the college chapel, or at one of the Churches, at the discretion of the President.

ART 4. No resident pupil shall be permitted to absent herself at any time from the college, without the consent of the President, and shall then, in all cases, be accompanied by a resident Professor or Teacher, or such other person as the President may approve of.

ART 5. If the parent or guardian of any resident pupil shall desire his or her daughter or ward to be permitted to visit families in the city or neighborhood, such a parent or guardian shall express in writing such wish, indicating particularly the families or places where such pupil shall be permitted to visit, and whether such visits shall be by night or day, or both: Provided, that such permission or authority shall not supersede the general power of the President to prohibit visits in all cases when in his judgment they would be improper.

ART 6. Pupils who do not reside with parents or guardians in the city of Columbia or its vicinity shall be required to board within the walls of the college.

ART 7. The students shall be furnished with the two text-books of their several classes at their own expense, but in no case shall the purchase of these or other articles for them be made a source of profit to any officer of the institution.

ART 8. Pupils are forbidden to open any accounts in the city of Columbia, except upon the written permission of parents or guardians.

DEPARTMENTS OF INSTRUCTION.

Roman Literature, Mathematics, Natural Philosophy, Logic, Mental and Moral Philosophy, Evidences of Christianity, Belles Lettres, Rhetoric, History, Geography, Astronomy, Chemistry, Mineralogy, Geology, Physiology, Modern Languages, Painting and Drawing, Music, (Vocal and Instrumental), Fancy Work.

CLASSES.

There shall be four Classes in the college, to be recognized by the usual names of Senior, Junior, Sophomore, and Primary.

COMPOSITIONS.

The members of the Senior, Junior, and Sophomore Classes will be required to prepare and submit, monthly, to the President, original essays or compositions, which shall be examined by the Faculty and Teachers, and their several merits noted.

SESSION.

There shall be one session annually of nine months, which shall commence on the first Wednesday in October, and terminate on the last Wednesday in June—the vacation extending from the latter date, to the first Wednesday in October. One week shall be allocated to Christmas holidays.

ADMISSION.

Board and tuition will in all cases be required, for each half session, in advance, and no applicant shall be admitted a student in college until this law shall have been complied with.

BOARD OF VISITORS.

There shall be a Board of Visitors, consisting of five gentlemen, who shall be appointed annually by the Board, and invited to attend the examination of the classes next preceding the close of each sessions.

EXAMINATION.

Any student, who shall refuse to undergo the examinations required by the college Laws, shall forfeit her standing in her class, unless for a sufficient reason she shall have been excused by the President.

COMMENCEMENT.

The Commencement Exercises shall be held annually on the last Wednesday in June, at which time diplomas will be granted and honors conferred.

ROOMS, HOW ASSIGNED.

The rooms shall be assigned to students by the President, and no change of rooms will be permitted without his consent.

VISITATION OF ROOMS.

The rooms of pupils shall at all times be subject to the visits and inspection of the Female Instructors and Matron, whose duty it shall be to report to the President any habitual want of neatness and order therein.

PUPILS TO KEEP ROOMS IN ORDER.

The students are required to put their rooms in order before breakfast of every morning, and to wait upon themselves in all things proper.

RATES OF BOARD AND TUITION.

For Board, including Washing, Lights, &c., with Tuition in English and the Classics, per Scholastic Year $200.00 Music, Piano and Harp, each, with use of instrument included 50.00 Guitar 40.00 French 40.00 Drawing, including colored crayon 40.00 Painting in oil colors and Pastel 50.00 Vocal Music 5.00 For Day Scholars, the rate of Tuition, per scholastic year, will be as follows:

First Graduating Class, 1860. Members: Lucie Allen (Mrs. Darlington); Fannie Beverly (Mrs. Crowder); Sallie Bryce; Rosalie Dantzler; Sarah Gamewell (Mrs. M.W. Heath); Harriet Glaze (Mrs. F.A. Burrows); Mary Jenkins; Aurie Jeter; Eliza Murchison; E.W. Oliver (Mrs. E.W. Brock); Virginia Shuler (Mrs. W.A. Black); Louisa Sterns (Mrs. M. Patterson); Ophelia Weems.

- For the Senior and Junior Classes, each $50.00
- For the Sophomore and Primary 40.00 Proportional deductions made for those who enter after the session has commenced; but such deduction shall not be made for less time than a week. Each pupil will be required to furnish her own bed-linen and towels.

CHAPTER 2—THE CIVIL WAR YEARS

College leaders witnessed a dramatic increase in enrollment during the Civil War years, with parents undoubtedly viewing the college as a safe haven for their daughters and perhaps a place to prepare them for new roles after the war. The college remained open until February 17, 1865, when the city of Columbia surrendered to the army of General William T. Sherman. Columbia Female College survived the fire that accompanied Sherman's capture of the city, and in the weeks and months following, homeless and destitute city residents found shelter in the vacant college dormitory rooms. The college closed in the years immediately following the Civil War, its future uncertain.

RECOLLECTIONS OF SALLIE ROGERS DRAKE, CLASS OF 1865[2]

At this time the college was crowded to its fullest capacity. There were about 300 in the building and 100 day-students. While the college was a Methodist Institute, there were no restrictions as to denominational attendance; students of all denominations were received. Our college government was of a semi-military nature: we marched to and from all classes; when we wanted out in the city (which was once each week only), we marched in double-file accompanied by three teachers, with the same order when we went to walk each afternoon.

We had two hydrants of city (or river) water on each floor, one at each end of the hall, basins and pitchers in each room. Drinking water (the city water being unfit for drinking) was retrieved from a well in the yard. Our food during the war was necessarily rather poor in quality, as the Southern states were then under a strict and effective blockade. We had no luxuries at all. We had beef, sweet potatoes, corn bread, and molasses; parched rye was a substitute for coffee. We got very tired of this plain menu, but no one complained, for every girl felt that every sacrifice made was for the

---

2   Mrs. Sallie Rogers Drake, Class of 1865, *Southern Christian Advocate*, August 14, 1919.

cause we all loved and that all sacrifices were made that the boys at the front might have more comfort. We wore dresses made of homespun, made over from mothers' or sisters' old dresses; occasionally some lucky girl got a calico dress (which cost ten dollars a yard in Confederate currency). When a brother or cousin visited us, how we enjoyed it! It was surprising how many cousins the girls had in those days.

The college closed very hurriedly in February 1865, on account of Sherman's approach to Columbia. He was about forty miles from Columbia when I left the college about Feb. 1, 1865. There was lots of excitement in the college then. We got away from Columbia as soon as possible. We heard of the wantonness and cruelties of Sherman's army and wished to get as far as possible from the path of his march.

RECOLLECTIONS OF PRESIDENT HENRY M. MOOD[3]

Henry M. Mood became president of Columbia College in 1863, in the midst of the Civil War. A Methodist minister, Mood had previously served as president of Davenport Female College in Lenoir, North Carolina, and succeeded William M. Martin in the Columbia Female College presidency. In early February 1864 Mood received a request from Confederate authorities to vacate the college property so that it could be used as a hospital. Mood maintained that the college should remain open and offered the following rationale in his letter to General PGT Beauregard.

The college was never so well patronized as during the war. Florida, Virginia, Georgia and Charleston, South Carolina, together with other portions of the State, contributed 200 boarders in the college building and more than 100 day scholars from the city of Columbia. Each of the small dormitories were provided with two bedsteads, the usual size bedstead being provided with a trundle bedstead to be rolled under the larger one during the day so as to economize room.

The music department had more than hundred pupils, and the art department was correspondingly well patronized.

Toward the close of the fourth year of the war, the state college buildings, which were used as a hospital, were deemed insufficient for the sick and wounded soldiers, and the Confederate authorities determined to establish another hospital in Columbia, and that either the asylum for the insane or the Methodist College building must be made to serve this purpose. Never did a man work harder than did the president of the college to thwart this purpose:

---

3   Henry M. Mood, "Columbia Female College During the War," *Southern Christian Advocate*, March 7, 1890.

personal effort, petition and remonstrance were used, but all to no avail. The president of the Board of Trustees gave permission to the military to take the building, the teachers and pupils were hurried off, and the president of the college saw the last quota depart on the final trip of the South Carolina railroad, for a part of the railroad was torn up by the Northern army the next day.

The building, thus appropriated, was placed in the charge of the Mrs. Herriot, and one barrel of whiskey and two crates of bedclothes were sent there; nothing more was done to establish a hospital. Soon after the departure of the president from the college building, Mrs. Herriot left. The college at this time was plainly but comfortably furnished, especially in mattresses, spreads and blankets, and there was wood in the yard amounting to one hundred cords. The books for the three hundred girls formed quite a library.

General Sherman, with his invading hosts, approached the city of Columbia, reaching the Broad River about the twelfth of February, 1865. Nothing could exceed the terror of the inhabitance, composed almost entirely of women and children, with a few old and disabled men, during these days and nights in which the city was bombarded. General Sherman made proclamation that private property would be respected, and that a guard would be furnished for each dwelling when applied for. Determining to avail myself of this offer as the president of the college, I sought one.

We were very happy in securing our guard, and felt quite safe under the eyes of his protection; that night for the first time in three we went to bed, all but Mrs. M., who could not consent to lie down. I had just gotten to sleep when she suddenly awoke me, declaring that the whole city was on fire. Seeing a circle of fire all around, and Main Street in a blaze from one end to the other, I at once awoke the guard, who was sleeping in a comfortable bed we had provided for him, and told him that the city was on fire. He came out and looked around and remarked that it was a fearful site, but said it was only what we might had expected under the circumstances, as South Carolina the first State to secede, and Columbia was the capital of the State. I asked him if General Sherman had given any order for the burning of Columbia. He said no; but that it was understood by the army that this city would be burned, because it was the capital of South Carolina and the "ordinance of Secession" had been first passed there.

After the departure of the army, the "sisters," who had charge of a Roman Catholic seminary in the city and had been burned out, went into the college building, taking possession of the third and a part of the second story, with the furniture, bedding, books and slates. Several families of citizens moved in the other half of the second story and the first. The large quantity of wood in the yard was cut and stacked in the entry ways and rooms, which was all consumed by the refugees. The pianos were taken by different citizens, and the large quantity of provisions saved was sold for Confederate money at private sale, when it was worth nothing, so that when the Trustees attempted to resuscitate the college they found that all that was left to the college, with a few exceptions, was the college building.

A PROFESSOR SAVES THE COLLEGE[4]

One of the stories handed down in the Columbia College tradition is that the college escaped the torch of Sherman's army through the efforts of faculty member W. H. Orchard. Orchard joined the faculty in 1859 and taught in the Music Department. Evelyn Barksdale Winn's history of the college, written as a master's thesis at the University of South Carolina in 1927, traces the origin of the story to a Columbia College alumna.

Mrs. J.C. Campbell, a student after the re-opening of the college (1873), says the college buildings were saved by W.H. Orchard, music teacher. Hearing of Sherman's proclamation that every empty house would be burned by a certain hour, Mr. Orchard left his own home and hastened to the college. He was forced to climb in the back window but succeeded in opening the front door from the inside. As he stood in the doorway he saw flames wreathing the city.

PRESIDENT MOOD STATES THE CASE FOR COLUMBIA FEMALE COLLEGE[5]

My dear Sir:

Last night I received a verbal message from Maj. Rhett [sic] through Mr. T. Walker, requiring the Columbia Female College to be vacated forthwith for hospital purposes, so as to give possession by Monday morning, with a statement that he has a positive order from you to impress the building. I returned answer to this remarkable demand, that I would not vacate the building, but would defend it and the young ladies under my care with the means which heaven has given me. This Sir, is one of a series of assaults to which we have been subjected for the past two years. We lost several students two years ago by a threat of impressments, these threats have continued ever since, and about two weeks ago a requisition was served upon our building, giving us 10 hours of day-light in which to vacate, and threatening us with having 600 sick soldiers moved

---

4 Evelyn Barksdale Winn, "A History of Columbia College," master's thesis, University of South Carolina, 1927, p. 28.
5 Letter in Columbia College Archives.

in upon us at that time. Our building was then full of young ladies. By a personal appeal to Gen. Hardee this proceeding was stopped, but we are subject to the same annoyance, and we now confidently appeal to you, to give us an Exemption for our building, for the following reasons.

A view from the State House looking north on Main Street following the burning of Columbia in 1865.

1st. Ours is a chartered college, of high grade of scholarship, with a larger patronage than any institution of similar grade in the South.

2nd. It is the representative Institution of the Methodist Church in South Carolina, and these series of attacks upon their favorite institution is only one form of attack upon Methodism.

3rd. The college was never more flourishing than when the late requisition was made upon it, two weeks ago.

4th. Our prospects are now encouraging, having received fifteen students in the last three day [sic], with several applications for others.

5th. We have a number of pupils who are refugees and have no home.

6th. I learn from the best authority, that with all the fighting about Richmond but one building has ever been impressed for hospital there, that the policy has been by timely preparation to prevent any necessity for impressments.

7th. The necessity which is now pled, if such exists, is from the want of forecast and enterprise on the part of the medical department, and shall we be held accountable for their delinquency? The ladies of Columbia with the assistance of the government have in a very short time, put up a building capable of holding many more sick soldiers than ours & much better adapted to the purpose, and the firm of Evans & Cogswell of this place have in an incredible short period erected a brick building capable of holding five times as many sick soldiers as ours.

If private enterprise can do this, cannot the Medical department, by a little foresight make all necessary provision for their sick?

8th. If our coast should be given up, our armies concentrated and Columbia becomes a base for military operations, with the loss already of two of our Female Institutions now in the hands of our government; there is an additional reason why the few which remain should be protected.

9th. Our young men cannot be educated, is it the purpose of those in authority to destroy the means of educating our young ladies?

An instrument of Exemption will greatly oblige the undersigned, the board of Trustees, and the Methodists of South Carolina. Please find with this Catalogue of the college.

Yours most respectfully,

Henry M. Mood

Pres. Columbia Female College

CHAPTER 3—THE NEW SOUTH

I n the years immediately following the Civil War, Columbia Female College was rented out for use as a hotel while college trustees and conference leaders struggled to find ways to settle the college's debts. So dire was the college's position that trustees and supporters faced a conference resolution in 1872 to sell the college property to pay off its creditors. Conference leaders wisely defeated the resolution, launching efforts to reduce the debt and secured bonds to reopen the college.

RE-ESTABLISHING THE SCHOOL

In 1873 the trustees appointed Reverend Samuel B. Jones, who had purchased the Spartanburg Female College in bankruptcy, as Columbia College's new president. Closing his Spartanburg campus and bringing his faculty and several students to Columbia, Jones reopened the Columbia Female College in January 1873.

Leadership changes in 1876 resulted in the appointment of the college's first layman, Dr. James Louis Jones, as president. In 1879 the trustees "leased" the college to Dr. Jones in an arrangement that provided free tuition for the daughters of Methodist ministers and a $20 fee to the president for each boarding student when the total enrollment reached

President Samuel B. Jones

55 students. Jones implemented a preparatory department for younger students and new vocational courses in teaching and telegraphy that held the promise of employment for graduates. Enrollment increased from 105 students, in 1879, to 172 in 1880. Dr. Jones recalled:

[O]ne day, unexpectedly to me, an officer of the Columbia Female College arrived in Cokesbury and approaching me without ceremony said the Trustees of the Columbia Female College had elected me as the President of that Institution and would I accept. Nothing could have been more unexpected for I had made no application for the place. I accepted the position to take effect at the opening of the ensuing scholastic year in the fall of 1876....

President J.L. Jones

It is proper to state just here that I found the college in a very embarrassed condition. By bad management the patronage was small and the college was $17,000 in debt and the Sheriff's hammer was about to fall on it and crush out the last vestige of life remaining in it. Besides this, the previous session under my predecessor had closed just two weeks before the commencement should have come off, which was caused by an alarm occasioned by the occurrence of several cases of typhoid fever in the college. Some of which proved fatal. The entire faculty resigned, the students fled and as in a storm at sea, a panic ensued and the vessel was left alone to go down amid the breakers. Had I known the true state of affairs before accepting the Presidency, doubtless I would have hesitated, but having once thrown my banner to the breeze, I am the last man at any time or anywhere to take it down. Just then I learned why I had been so unanimously elected. They said they had heard that I had been successful in resurrecting dead colleges and, as in all desperate cases this college needed just such heroic treatment as was incident to my practice....

I was with this college five years during which I won the grandest triumph of my life. In the face of rivalry and bitter competition, I alleged alarm as to sickness, restored the public confidence, satisfied the Sheriff, filled the house with pupils, paid six or seven thousand dollars of the college debt, made for myself four to five thousand dollars each year clear all expense, and at the close of my Presidency left the college with two thousand pupils, the largest in the state and with a reputation before unknown and upon which to this day it floats.

STABILITY INCREASES AND UNPLANNED RENOVATIONS

An important measure of stability emerged in the 1880s with appointment of Reverend Osgood Andrew Darby, a member of the South Carolina Conference, as president in

President Osgood Andrew Darby

1881. With Darby's appointment the college's "lease" arrangement was terminated, and the institution returned to direct control by the conference. Darby immediately began to focus conference attention on the institution and led efforts to steadily improve the college finances.

The Trustees tapped former president Samuel B. Jones to lead the college in 1890, a position Jones held until he decided because of failing health to step aside in 1894. Reverend John A. Rice, a prominent member of the South Carolina Conference, assumed the college presidency as the institution entered its final years in the nineteenth century. Under Rice's leadership the college was transformed from what historian Evelyn Barksdale Winn described as "mainly a finishing school for young ladies, with a curriculum little advanced over a high school" to "a real college, its course of study equal to that of men's college's."[6]

In January 1895 the college experienced its first fire, which damaged a significant portion of its west wing. The campus was renovated, and hot and cold water were now made available to dormitory students. The conference passed a resolution in 1895 designating the second Sunday in March as Columbia Female College Day and urged each church to provide a program on the college and to take a special offering for its support. As the college prepared to enter the new century, it enjoyed a full dormitory enrollment, an improved curriculum, a sound financial base, and an alumnae association dedicated to its future.

ACTIVISM ON AND OFF THE CAMPUS

President Darby's administration coincided with the rise of southern women's new interest for expanding social roles. This path of women's social activism first began with the establishment of women's religious societies and soon led to concerns with social ills, educational improvement, and ultimately woman's suffrage. In late 1878 Methodist women in South Carolina became the first denominational

President John A. Rice, D.D.

group to organize themselves into a statewide organization, the Women's Missionary Society. A number of the college's early graduates joined this organization, assuming new and highly visible leadership activities in service to church activities around the

---

6   Evelyn Barksdale Winn, "A History of Columbia College."

state; a local campus chapter was also organized.

Minnie Melton attended Columbia Female College in the years just following its reopening after the Civil War. Her interests and activities reflected new avenues for women's civic participation in the post-war South. Following her marriage to University of South Carolina professor Dr. William B. Burney, she began an active involvement with newly emerging women's organizations on the local, state and national level. She was a key leader in the women's club movement in Columbia and South Carolina. Mrs. Burney served as one of the early presidents of the South Carolina Federation of Women's Clubs, as state regent for the South Carolina Daughters of the American Revolution (DAR), and as a national officer of the DAR. In the early 20th century she led efforts to establish a residential center for young working women who had relocated to Columbia.

Minnie Melton Burney, Class of 1876, attended Columbia Female College in the years just following its reopening after the Civil War.

Without question, the most significant national organization for women in the 1880s was the Women's Christian Temperance Union (WCTU) founded by Frances Willard, a Methodist women's advocate in Illinois. Columbia Female College graduate and Laurens County native Mary Yeargin served as an early leader in the South Carolina Women's Temperance Union, the first statewide chapter organized in the South.

Yeargin exemplified the great promise and talent of well-educated women in South Carolina in the last decades of the nineteenth century. She was the valedictorian of her graduating class in 1885, and was offered a faculty position in the English Department at the college. In 1890 she was tapped by Governor Benjamin R. Tillman as one of three commissioners to canvass the state in order to determine the need for a state-supported college for women, which resulted in the establishment of Winthrop College. Following her work with this commission, she enrolled at Cornell University for graduate study in law. Her life was cut short in 1893 when she drowned in a boating accident at Cornell. Fellow Laurens County native and Columbia College alumna Dr. Wil Lou Gray later observed, "Thus was cut short the life of one of the most capable of the leaders of women of her day...."

A prominent Methodist women's leader and former president of a Methodist woman's college, Frances Willard became a key founder of the Woman's Christian Temperance Union, the largest women's organization in the country in the late 1880s. She visited the Columbia College campus in the 1880s and students organized The Willard Society in her honor.

Eloise Welch Wright, class of 1892, provides another example of the activism of many Columbia Female College graduates. In the years immediately following her graduation, she was employed as a teacher until her marriage in 1900 to businessman Robert Downs Wright of Newberry County, S.C. She became the mother of two children of her own and two stepchildren. Wright became a charter member of both the Newberry Woman's Club and the Newberry Civic League; an active leader in the Daughters of the American Revolution and the United Daughters of the Confederacy; a life member and past president of the Women's Society of Christian Service; and a board member of Central Methodist Church for more than 30 years. In 1963 she was chosen "Newberry County Woman of the Year."

Mary Yeargin

Eloise Welch Wright

FOUNDATION OF THE ALUMNAE ASSOCIATION

In June 1882 Columbia Female College graduates formed their own women's network: the Columbia Female College Alumnae Association was organized under the presidency of Janie Herbert Haynes, an 1876 graduate and a charter member of the South Carolina Women's Missionary Society, when a number of graduates gathered in the college parlor on June 21. The purpose, as set forth in the constitution of the association, was to keep members informed of old associates, to assist members in keeping up literary work, and to aid in the education of fatherless daughters. Dues for joining were 50 cents, but were soon increased to one dollar. In the early days, the association had an address or essay read by a member at each meeting. At the outset those who had not graduated were only associate members; in 1885 the constitution was changed so that any former pupil of the college might join the Association. In 1886 the association requested the Board of Trustees to recognize graduates of the old Spartanburg Female College as Alumnae of Columbia; this request was granted.

The first work which the Association undertook was raising money to refurnish the college dormitories. This was done by personal subscription from the Alumnae and their friends. In 1889, at the suggestion of Miss Helen McMaster (Class of 1875) of Columbia, plans were begun to establish a scholarship of $40.00

Janie Herbert Haynes and family.

a year.

This association, which initially met annually during commencement week, became the fifth such organization of women's college graduates in the country—following Elmira, Vassar, Wellesley, and Smith colleges—and the South's first. It played a critical role in establishing and maintaining a network of Columbia Female College women who kept in contact with one another and were actively involved in addressing the needs of their alma mater.

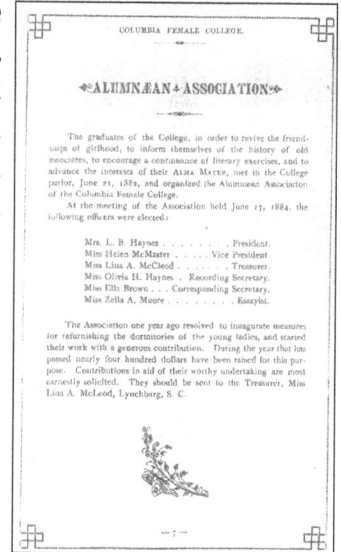

From the Columbia Female College Catalogue, 1883–84.

ADDENDUM: EXCERPTS FROM THE
COLLEGE CATALOGUE, 1881–1882[7]

The Fall Session will commence Wednesday, September 13, 1882. The President, with a full and efficient corps of teachers, an improved course of study, a high standard of scholarship, and good domestic arrangements, offers all that is necessary for the higher education of the daughters of our people. Special attention will be given to thorough instruction, to the religious training of pupils, to the improvement of health, to the formation of character, and to the cultivation of manners.

GOVERNMENT.

The government of the college will be mild and parental in its character. Rules will be furnished to each pupil upon entrance, but they will not interfere with the freedom of the pupil any more than is necessary to good order and safety. It will be the earnest endeavor of the Faculty to develop such an appreciation of feminine excellence and love of moral rectitude that the pupils will largely govern themselves. Discipline will be maintained, but the fact is recognized that it is better to win a cheerful than force a reluctant obedience.

BOARDING DEPARTMENT.

This department is under the care of the President and his wife, with a polite and competent assistant.

The table will be neat, and supplied with good, well-cooked, wholesome food, and in as great variety as the market affords.

No effort will be spared to surround the pupils with the gentle and refining influences of the best home life.

THE COLLEGE BUILDINGS.

This is one of the most elegant and imposing structures which has been erected for educational purposes in the State. Located in our central city, it offers peculiar advantages to patrons. It can be reached by rail from nearly every part of the State in a few hours and at small expense. It is situated on a wide and beautifully shaded street, within convenient distance to churches and business houses, and yet so retired as to be free from the noise and bustle of the city. It is furnished with a system of conduits

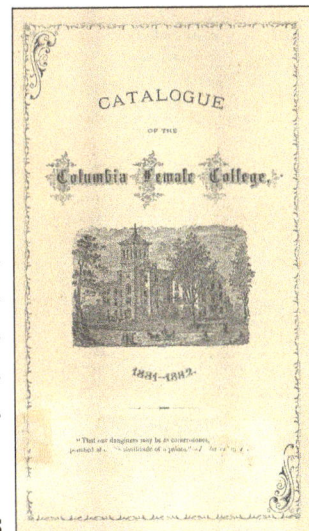

---

7   Columbia College Archives.

for conveying gas and water to each story.

HEALTHFULNESS.

One of the chief recommendations of the college is its healthfulness. Columbia, as demonstrated by statistics, is one of the healthiest cities in the south. In addition to Calisthenics in the college Chapel, the pupils are required to take daily exercise in the open air when the weather permits. Though hundreds have been educated here, there has been but one death among pupils since the college was opened. In case of sickness the college physician will be called and parents immediately notified. Parents may rest assured that no effort will be spared to preserve the health of those committed to our care.

Students in 1879.

EXAMINATIONS.

In the Preparatory Department the classes will be examined frequently. In the Collegiate Department before any text book can be laid aside there shall be a thorough written and oral examination. At the close of the session the pupils of the whole school will be required to pass a similar examination. These examinations are not designed to be exhibitions, but are to improve the pupils and to assist the teachers in marketing their progress.

Pupils who fail to obtain an average grade of seventy in a scale of one hundred will not be advanced to a higher study.

LIBRARY AND READING ROOM.

The college has not been supplied with a library, though the President has a private library of a thousand or twelve hundred volumes, to which the students will have access.

Our Reading Room is furnished with magazines, Illustrated Weeklies, and the leading papers of the State, both religious and secular.

MONTHLY LECTURES.

The first Friday of each month will be devoted to a lecture in the college chapel on some subject in Ethics, History, Biography, Art, Literature, or Science. Different gentlemen will be invited for these occasions.

Students of the 1875–76 school year.

Music will be furnished by the teachers and pupils. They will be open to patrons and a few invited guests.

SOCIETIES.

The Wightman and Willard Literary Societies are doing much to develop the powers and improve the taste of the pupils. Their halls are tastefully fitted up and are furnished with small but select libraries.

In addition to these the young ladies have organized a College Missionary Society, which is auxiliary to the Women's Missionary Society of the South Carolina Conference, and a Temperance Society, which is called the Chapin Temperance Union.

Students in 1876.

UNIFORM.

Young ladies boarding in the college will be required, when they appear in public, to adopt the following uniform:

- FOR WINTER.—Black dress, trimmed with black; black cloak, black hat, trimmed according to taste.
- FOR SPRING AND SUMMER.—Plain white muslin or lawn; plain hat, trimmed according to taste. For common use, a plain straw hat.
- FOR NIGHT EXHIBITIONS AND OTHER OCCASIONS.—Linen, lawn or tarlatan; white or colored may be worn.

These regulations do not apply to those who are in mourning.

Winter uniforms should be provided when the pupil enters in September; Spring by the 15th of April.

Dresses should be made at home. Too much time and money are absorbed if made here.

Parents are urged to discourage extravagant dressing at Commencement.

PUPIL'S OUTFIT.

Each young lady must furnish her toilet articles, one white counterpane, two blankets, one pair of sheets, one pair pillow cases, six towels, six doilies, one doily ring, umbrella and overshoes. Each of these articles, as well as all pieces of clothing, should be plainly marked with owner's name.

The student body in 1899.

Addendum: Scale of Demerits in the Columbia Female College

The activities and behavior of Columbia Female College students were carefully monitored throughout the early history of the institution. Parents were kept well informed of their daughters' deportment as well as of their academic progress.

No.	REPORTS.	Demerits.
1	Absence from Prayers, Recitation or Church	5
2	Absence from Chapel at Study Hours	3
3	Absence from Music Rooms at Practice Hours	3
4	Absence from Open Air Exercises	3
5	Improper Conduct at Prayers, Recitation, or in Chapel	5
6	Improper Conduct in Dining Room	3
7	Improper Conduct in Church, or any Public Place	10
8	Defacing Building or Furniture	3
9	Using Musical Instruments except at Lesson and Practice Hours	
10	Neglecting to Close Musical Instrument After the last Practice Hour	
11	Neglecting to Turn Off the Gas After the Last Practice Hour	3
12	Sitting in, or Throwing Anything from, a Window	1
13	Speaking Aloud from a Window	3
14	Neglecting to Keep Room in Order	3
15	Dancing in Building	6
16	Leaving Room After Retiring Bell	3
17	Neglecting to Extinguish Fire at Night	6
18	Neglecting to Extinguish Fire in Day Time	4
19	Tardiness in Obeying the Bells	3
20	Visiting While on Sick List	3
21	Disorderly Conduct in the Building	
22	Leaving Chapel or Recitation Room	
23	Moving from one Room to Another	
24	Communications by Signs or Gestures from any part of the Building or Premises with a Gentleman on the Street	10 to 25
25	Disrespect to any Officer or Teacher	10 to 25
26	Clandestine Correspondence	10 to 25
27	Accepting Attentions from Young Gentlemen	10 to 25
28	Leaving College Premises	10 to 100
29	Other Offenses or Improprieties	1 to 100

Scale of Demerits from the Columbia Female College Catalogue of 1884.

ADDENDUM: REQUIREMENTS FOR ADMISSION, 1897[8]

Candidates for admission to the Freshman Class are examined on the following subjects:

- English.—Complete grammar, including the writing of the simpler forms of literary production. The pupil is expected to be familiar with the parts of speech, forms of words, their construction, and the analysis of the sentence. Parsing is stressed. It is suggested to those preparing for college that they do a great deal of drill work. They should also read as many English classics as practicable.
- Latin.—Three books of Caesar and the grammar. The pupil must be able to translate simple English prose into Latin.
- History.—History of the United States and of South Carolina.
- Mathematics.—The whole of Arithmetic and of Algebra.
- Natural Science.—Physical Geography and Physiology.

Applicants for higher classes are examined on all the work below the class for which they apply.

Diploma of Lucile Ellerbe, Class of 1888.

---

8   Columbia College Archives.

CHAPTER 4—AN ERA OF CHANGE

The first half of the 20th century was a period of change and transition for Columbia College. Waves of institutional successes, including a new home and modern facility in north Columbia and accreditation by prestigious educational associations, alternated with events of near-tragic proportions. The beautiful new facility, opened in 1905, was destroyed by a devastating fire in 1909, and the rebuilt Columbia College confronted economic depression and financial instability that almost closed its doors. With each step forward, new threats always seemed to loom. And, yet, Columbia College continued to strive ahead, ultimately surviving an institutional merger that undermined its autonomy and placed its future at great risk.

A NEW CAMPUS AND FACILITY

To be certain, Columbia College entered the new century with optimism and renewed commitment to its special mission in higher education. As the nineteenth century ended, enrollment swelled at the campus on Plain (Hampton) Street and campus leaders sensed that the existing facility was not adequate to serve an increasing number of young women. Originally designed for some 100 boarding students, college officials found ways to accommodate as many as 125 or even 130 students, but other qualified applicants had to be turned away.

In 1901, the Board of Trustees asked the Methodist Conference for the authority to relocate the campus to a larger site. Conference leaders approved the request but reserved the authority to make the final determination of the new location. In 1902, a Board of Trustees committee reported to the conference on potential locations: in Lexington County, Sumter, Laurens, and Greenwood. Conference leaders maintained that the college's charter required that it be located in Columbia and by a vote of 120 to 94 the decision was made to remain in Columbia. In 1903, F.H. Hyatt of Columbia offered 20 acres of land in the suburbs of the city, along with a $5000 cash contribution toward construction.

Frederick Hargrave Hyatt.

The Board of Trustees accepted F.H. Hyatt's offer and the offer of an adjacent twenty acres by John T. Sloan, and construction soon began. In April 1905, the cornerstone was laid in full Masonic ceremonies, with a marble block that officially removed the word "female" from the college's name. The new facility was opened in October 1905.

The college was situated about two miles north of the city, within 15 minutes' ride of the State Capitol. Easily accessible from all parts of the state, its location was ideal for a college. The buildings were large, well-ventilated, well-appointed brick structures, heated by steam, lighted by electricity, and abundantly supplied with purest water. Two students were assigned to a room. No institution for the education of young women in the South surpassed Columbia College in the convenience, comfort, and attractions of its buildings, or in the beauty and accessibility of its location. Bathrooms, with hot and cold water and water-closets, were conveniently arranged on every floor and in both wings of this magnificent building.

The administration building was the central edifice, containing the offices, parlors, classrooms, library, reading-room, and the handsomely furnished halls of the Wightman and Carlisle Literary Societies. A third story was added giving additional classrooms and a

Columbia College campus, 1905–1909.

handsome art studio. All rooms opened either to the outside or in the open court, thus making every room an outside room, receiving the light of the sun during a portion of every day.

West of the administration building, and connected with it and the dormitories, was the swimming pool and the gymnasium, a handsome two-story structure, built and equipped for the use of the students. East of the administration building, and connected with it and the dormitories, in the same way, is the beautiful two-story building containing well-equipped science halls and the Business department. The spacious dining hall, with capacity for seating 400 students, was on the first floor with access from the dormitories, the administration building, or the open courts. In rear of this space were pantries, cold storage rooms, and kitchen. Besides the sleeping rooms, the second floor housed several classrooms and an elegant auditorium, with a seating capacity of 900. In the rear of the chapel practice rooms were located, thus placing the musical instruments away from the recitation and sleeping rooms. The campus comprised 20 acres, the whole of which was enjoyed by the students for outdoor games and open-air exercises.

Faculty *of* Columbia College

W. W. DANIEL, A. M., D. D., PRESIDENT,
Greek Language and Literature.

MRS. K. R. BECKWITH, A. M., LADY PRINCIPAL
English Bible.

MRS. M. B. COFIELD, A. M.,
History and Political Economy.

MRS. N. B. McDOWELL, A. M.,
English Language and Literature.

MISS KATHERINE HUDGENS, A. B.,
Assistant English Language and Literature.

MISS PENELOPE McDUFFIE, A. M.,
Latin Language and Literature.

MISS NELLE B. LOWE, A. M.,
Modern Languages and Literature.

MISS JANE WELLS COLSON, S. B.,
Natural Science.

G. T. PUGH, A. M., PH. D.,
Mathematics and Astronomy.

MISS I. D. MARTIN,
Mental and Moral Science.

MISS SALLIE M. ALSTON,
Business Department.

MISS SARAH PECK HINES,
Expression and Physical Culture.

MISS CAROLINE LEWIS,
Art

W. G. UTERMOEHLEN,
Director of Music Department.

MRS. ADAH D. MERKELEY,
Piano

MISS JEAN ADGER FLINN,
Piano

MISS LUCY HAMER,
Piano

MISS LOUISE HUGHES,
Voice.

COLLEGE SCHOOL.

MISS MARY ELIZA McLEOD, A. B.,
English and History.

MISS LOUISE GLENN, A. B.,
Latin and Mathematics.

MISS SARAH PECK HINES,
Science.

11

The Columbia College faculty of 1906.

STARTING OVER AGAIN

In 1900 Reverend William Wellington Daniel, a native of Laurens County and graduate of Newberry College, assumed the college presidency and began a 16-year term of office until 1916. Married to Columbia College graduate Rowena Aull, Class of 1882, Daniel was a passionate advocate for women's higher education and oversaw the move to the new campus in north Columbia. He also helped the college recover from the destruction of the facility by fire in 1909, and following that he directed its subsequent rebuilding, and the strengthening of the academic program and curriculum. Dean D.D. Peele offered the following tribute to his work on the occasion of the Alumnae Association's Portrait Dedication for Dr. Daniel in 1946.

President W.W. Daniel.

"Institutions are built by many people. Dr. William Wellington Daniel has and will ever have a prominent place among the builders of Columbia College.... He became president of the college at forty-one and resigned at fifty-seven, thus giving to this institution the sixteen choice years of his life. When asked to summarize his work for the college in a few words, one who knew him well replied, "He did much with little."

Dr. Daniel oversaw the opening of the new campus in 1905. Just four years later, a fire left the college president severely burned and destroyed the new facility. The college's insurance policy was woefully insufficient to cover the loss, and fundraising initiatives were launched to rebuild the campus. The State newspaper reported on April 9, 1909:

> All that is left of Columbia College today is the bare, fire burnt walls, fire having gutted all of the buildings with the exception of the power house at the early hour to-day. The loss is over $200,000, and the insurance $85,000. The fire was caused by a defective electric wire; it is stated, in the west wing of the group of buildings, and spread rapidly to the others.

Alice Rowena Aull Daniel, Class of 1882

Although no definite plans for the future have been announced, it is assured that the college will open on September 23, and all students are expected to be present.

Dr. W.W. Daniel, the president of the school, is at the Colonia, suffering from several severe burns received while trying to extinguish fire....

Everything had recently been painted and varnished, and the oil carried the flames at a rapid pace, spreading to the main administration building, which was three stories high, science hall, dining room, music room, art studios, gymnasium and kitchen, sweeping everything before it. All of the bedrooms, over one hundred and fifty in number, were destroyed.

Remains of the college after the fire of 1909.

The new pipe organ in the auditorium, which had just been installed at a cost of over $5,000, was completely destroyed. Only one piano out of about thirty-five was saved from the music room. The power house, which cost $10,000, was not injured, also several cottages near the buildings. The papers of the college were secured by Dr. Daniel before leaving his office. All of the furniture of the school was lost.[9]

---

9   *The State*, April 9, 1909.

Following the devastation of the fire, the board determined to rebuild the college. President Daniel participated in fundraising to rebuild, and supervised the opening of the campus again in 1910. He recruited faculty who would hold special places of honor in the college's history, including David D. Peele, James Milton Ariail, and Georgia O'Keefe. He revamped the curriculum and raised the academic standards, and in 1911 Columbia College received the coveted "A" grade recognition by the Methodist Association of Colleges.

President Daniel and Students in 1904.

In 1916, upon the resignation of President Daniel, the Board of Trustees selected Dr. Griffith T. Pugh, the chairman of the college's Mathematics Department, as the institution's new president. A native of Prosperity, South Carolina, Pugh was a graduate of Wofford College and held a doctorate degree from Vanderbilt University. An able administrator, Pugh increased the enrollment substantially, reduced the college debt, and improved the campus facility.

President Griffith T. Pugh.

ECONOMIC STRUGGLES

Toward the end of the first decade of the 1900s, South Carolina experienced a serious economic depression as the price for cotton spiraled downwards, leaving the parents of many Columbia College students unable to pay for tuition and boarding costs. Determined that no student should be turned out and that the college must remain open, President Daniel informed the faculty that there were no funds to cover their salaries and requested their help. In an exemplary instance of dedication, faculty members reaffirmed their commitment to the ideals of the college and continued their duties without pay. As a measure of financial stability returned in the early 1920s, the crisis eased. It is without question, however, that the loyalty of the faculty enabled Columbia College to keep its doors open. Dr. Ariail recalled:

> Problems weighed heavily upon Dr. Daniel. Frequently late at night he would pace the long hall and drop into my study to unburden himself. One night he said in agony: "Ariail, the Methodist Church founded this college to educate its daughters and other women of the State. I have a college full of girls; their

parents are in financial distress and I do not intend to send one girl home because her parents cannot pay the college bills. I do not know how I can do it, but I will." And he did just that. I learned that he used much of his personal savings.

The financial situation of the college raised the question of how was the faculty to live. Mr. F.H. Hyatt and Dr. W.J. Murray, strong supporters of Dr. Daniel and the college, met with the faculty and frankly put the cards on the table. They said that the college was in no condition to pay salaries, but that these would be paid when obligations due it were realized. They also said that any member of the Faculty who felt that he or she could not face conditions would be released with understanding and sympathy. A number of teachers from out of the State withdrew, but Dr. Peele and I elected to stay, probably because we had no where else to go, and had the feeling that we would not starve.

Dr. Daniel assured the members of the Faculty that if they came upon an emergency, he would go on their note at the bank. On one occasion when I was in dire need, I went to him. He had accumulated some gold coins and he said he would lend me $50 in gold, if I promised to repay in gold. The president of the bank assured me that I could get $50 in gold at any time. I accepted the loan and long afterwards repaid it in gold.

Professor James Milton Ariail in 1923.

The spirit of the student body during these crucial days was an inspiration. It was a time of sharing. If a girl could not afford an evening dress (the Junior Reception still went on) or a suitable dress for church, the girls found these for the less fortunate, and no girl was embarrassed. It must also be remembered that the girls had mothers at home. Since there was no place to go, and little money to spend, the work of the college was intensified, effective, and up to standard, although the war took some faculty members from us.[10]

During that era, Dr. Ariail composed and published Columbia College's alma mater, capturing in song the spirit and tenacity of the institution and the people who comprised the community of the college:

---

10   J.M. Ariail, *Columbia College, 1912–1968*; Columbia College Archives.

We sing the praise of her we love,
We lift on high her name in song;
White as the gleaming stars above,
Columbia, mother, great and strong!
She who has been, shall ever be,
Wise, good and true eternally.
No stain shall touch the purity
Of our Columbia College.

Her virtues we acclaim today,
That all men might this of her deem;
Her mission is to light the way
With learning's clearest, sweetest gleam.
Her gentle heart has made her great,
Her breath is love, she knows no hate.
Her faith that God controls her fate
Makes brave our own Columbia!

The storms of years upon her beat,
But do not scar her loving face;
And fire has wrapped her in its heat,
But on her soul has left no trace.
The travails of her mother heart,
As from her side her daughters part—
We know then thy quick tears start,
Oh, gentle Alma Mater!

And here we pledge our love to thee,
No matter what the years may bring,
Or what in life our lot shall be,
Columbia, we thy glory sing!
We love thee for thy zealous care,
For lofty aims to thee so dear;
Our hearts shall ever breathe this prayer,
God keep our own Columbia![11]

STUDENT LIFE AND ALUMNAE INVOLVEMENT

Throughout the period, Columbia College students sought opportunities to experience

---

11   James Milton Ariail, 1916.

a greater independence on campus and frequently challenged the watchful eyes and authority of dormitory matrons and chaperones. In 1904 the senior class for the first time published an annual, called the *Columbian*, to be published in the spring of each year and offering commentary on college life, class histories, notes on clubs, and short

Columbia College Alma Mater with music scale.

stories and poems of the student body. In 1914 a tentative form of student government was first implemented on campus, and one year later Emma Jane Varn, Class of 1915, became the college's first student-government president. On a spring afternoon in 1914, students cut classes, left campus without a chaperone, and staged a woman's suffrage parade, later informing the college president that it was all just an "April Fool's" joke.

Georgia O'Keefe, one of the country's most important artists of the twentieth century, taught at Columbia College in 1915–1916. She later recalled of period that "it was an important time in my life and some of my most important drawings were made at Columbia College." She lived close to the Ariail family and painted a portrait of their daughter. Dr. Ariail later observed that "she was a young artist—ambitious, vivacious, and well on her way to becoming one of America's famous artists."

For students, membership in the institution's literary societies was an important component of campus life and provided a critical opportunity to develop leadership skills. The college's first societies appeared in the 1880s during an early wave of women's activism in the state, particularly among Methodist women who established women's societies within the conference. The college's two most important literary organizations in the early 1900s were the Carlisle Society and the Wightman Society. Student Elizabeth Louise Duncan (Mrs. J. Olin Horne), class of 1914, recalled:

Georgia O'Keefe, faculty member from 1915–16.

> Two societies awaited us when we entered the doors of the college, Wightman and Carlisle. Many of our number joined their forces to one or the other of these, but when it was finally decreed that each student must belong to some society, a third, named the Daniel Society, was organized. This was during our Freshman year. But gradually the new society withered and died. Things drifted on in this way until a society was again organized, the Woodrow Wilson Society. All three societies are now in a flourishing condition and an aid to the girls in their regular work.[12]

Columbia College alumnae increased their involvement in the life of their alma mater, raising funds for the rebuilding of the campus after the 1909 fire and securing books and furniture for the library. Alumnae funds also refurbished parlors and dormitory rooms, beautified the campus, and enhanced the endowment.

---

12 *The Columbian,* 1918.

44

CHAPTER 5—A TIME OF PROGRESS

In the years following the Great War, Columbia College found itself in a season of great progress, as well as a time of change and challenge. Changes in leadership and campus life, as well as the difficulties of the Depression era and World War II, affected the college deeply, leading the women of Columbia College to rise to new heights even as stability on the campus grew in many ways—not least, financially—and facilities expanded to meet increasing need. Passing through a significant 75th anniversary, the college demonstrated its endurance and longevity through a persevering spirit and the accomplishment of long-sought milestones.

LEADERSHIP CRISIS

In the spring of 1920, a student disciplinary matter resulted in a leadership crisis involving students, faculty, and friends of the institution. Dean Peele and Professor Ariail resigned over disagreement with President Pugh's decision to expel the students in question. The Board of Trustees ultimately requested Pugh's resignation in August 1920. Professor Ariail gave the following account:

> The college was running smoothly until the spring of 1920 when a most unhappy and critical situation arose. Five students, consisting of two Seniors and three Underclassmen, were walking around the block facing the college. At the corner they were passing a house in which lived a sixteen year old boy known to the girls and well-known around the campus. When he called to the girls that he had a new record he wanted them to hear, the girls went in, heard the record and probably danced a little; but remained only a short time. It happened that the boy was alone in the house at the time.
>
> The students were immediately summoned by the Lady Principal, who was a strict disciplinarian, and very influential with the President.

Charges were made against the girls, and after frequent meetings of the Faculty, a split Faculty voted expulsion for the Seniors, and suspension for the Underclassmen....

In June, the Board of Trustees met and overruled the action of the President and Faculty and ordered the students restored to full standing. The Faculty all along was divided... Professor Peele, feeling that he could no longer support the position of the President had resigned and accepted a position elsewhere. The student body met in the auditorium, demanded that the President and Faculty review the case of the students, and find a less severe penalty....

[A] meeting was called and efforts made to get some action, but the faculty was divided, the women were adamant in their convictions, and nothing was done. Thus, the situation moved into July with the action of the Board of Trustees still not accepted. In the meantime, Dr. J.L. Mann... Superintendent of the city schools of Greenville... insisted that the action of the Board of Trustees be carried out....

On the night of August 20, 1920, the Board of Trustees met. Dr. Pugh came to my home and requested minutes of the faculty meetings, and after a long discussion, he was asked if he intended to carry out the will of the Board. His answer was an emphatic NO! I was told later that at this point the Board voted the Presidency of Columbia College vacant....

Dr. Pugh was an able man, and I felt that he had been influenced by the persistent feeling of a majority of the Faculty women who believed that the

President J. Caldwell Guilds

college had been injured, and held to his first decision. There is no question as to his real contribution to Columbia College. Until the incident recounted, his administration moved forward, and the impact of his strong character and lovable qualities as a man, was lasting upon students and faculty.

After his retirement from Columbia College, Dr. Pugh went to Winthrop as Professor of Math, where he taught until his retirement.[13]

In 1920, J. Caldwell Guilds, then headmaster of the Carlisle School in Bamberg, was appointed Columbia College's new president. Dr. Guilds charted an ambitious plan for the institution, which led to the largest enrollments in the

13   J.M. Ariail, Columbia College Archives.

college's history at that point (414 in 1937), improvements in the physical plant, and a solid endowment. Early in his presidency he oversaw the completion of the main building on campus, the erection of the Vera Young Thomas Memorial Library, and the establishment of the "Little Chapel." Under his leadership the college was admitted to membership in the American Association of Colleges in 1934 and in the Southern Association of Colleges in 1938. Guilds became the longest-serving president of the college, stepping down in 1948, when Columbia College merged with Wofford.

The Vera Young Thomas Memorial Library.

ACCREDITATION AND ON-CAMPUS CHALLENGES

During both World Wars, Columbia College students joined women college students across the nation in Red Cross volunteer work, learning more about war, geography, and foreign relations. In 1945, undoubtedly reflecting a desire to become better informed about campus events and to offer their own perspective on campus matters, they organized and published a college newspaper, the *Post Script*, a publication now in its sixtieth year.

In the 1920s graduating classes began the practice of funding class gifts that included the fountain on the front campus. Seeking a more formal involvement in college affairs, the Alumnae Association passed a resolution in 1921 petitioning for representation on the college's governing board. In 1925 the conference appointed two alumnae representatives to the Board of Trustees—Wil Lou Gray, Class of 1903, and Mrs. Ivah Epps Frierson, Class of 1897. Heading in a more professional direction and wanting to expand its services, the association in 1926 hired its first director, Miss Emmie G. Wright, Class of 1912. These steps reflected the desire of Columbia College graduates to assume important roles in the life of the college and to provide financial support and other assistance for its mission. The highly visible work of Gray, the state's most prominent early-20th-century woman reformer, provided a model for alumnae activism and service.

The Alumnae Association, under Grays's leadership, also established an endowment of $50,000 for the school, announcing plans in 1925 for a gift at the 75th anniversary in 1929. This paralleled the administration's efforts under President Guilds's leadership to establish a permanent endowment for the school, which reached $100,000 in 1926 and continued to grow in anticipation of the pursuit of accreditation.

One of the most important chapters in the college history concerns the campaign to secure accreditation by the prestigious Southern Association of Schools and Colleges. Launched by President Guilds, this effort required that the college meet rigorous standards in a range of areas including academics, administration, curricular offerings, library holdings, and endowment. Under President Guilds's able leadership the college hired its first academic dean and its first dean of students, eliminated its preparatory department, opened its first freestanding library, and established its first significant endowment. In 1938 the college was admitted to the Southern Association.

NOTABLE PRESENCES ON CAMPUS, AND AN ABSENCE

Wil Lou Gray, a native of Laurens County, is one of Columbia College's most illustrious graduates. Entering the college at the turn of the twentieth century, she took an active role in campus life and became president of one of the two campus organizations, the Wightman Literary Society. Upon her graduation in 1903, she enrolled at Columbia University in New York and earned a master's degree in political science. In 1918, when South Carolina's illiteracy rate was estimated to be more than 25 percent of the population, Gray accepted an appointment as field representative for the South Carolina Illiteracy Commission. She launched the "Write Your Name" campaign, and began a lifelong effort to eradicate adult illiteracy that touched the lives of more than 30,000 South Carolinians. In 1948 she opened a permanent school with legislative appropriations, the South Carolina Opportunity School. A national leader in adult education, Gray received honorary degrees from virtually every college in the state, and she was honored in a joint session of the South Carolina General Assembly. She is one of just four women to be recognized with a portrait hanging in the South Carolina Capitol. Wil Lou Gray served as president of the Columbia College Alumnae Association in 1924–25 and was one of the first two women to serve on the college's Board of Trustees.

Wil Lou Gray, second from left, 1902.

David D. Peele joined the Columbia College faculty in 1907 as an English professor, but soon moved to become chair of the mathematics department. A graduate of Trinity College (Duke University), he earned a master's degree and completed additional graduate work at the University of Chicago. In 1920 he became Columbia College's first Academic Dean. He served as Dean for 29 years until his retirement in 1949. James Milton Ariail observed of Dean Peele that "he held the admiration of his faculty and students by his love of learning; his adherence to scholarship; by his keen sense of humor; by his frankness, and by his penetrating and logical mind.

Rev. Mason Crum of the South Carolina Conference joined the faculty in 1920 as professor of Biblical Literature and Religious Education. Professor Crum was a graduate of Wofford College and studied at the Divinity School of Vanderbilt University, as well as in the Harvard School of Philosophy. He taught in the Wofford Fitting School and served a year as principal of the Fort Motte High School. He came to the college from the pastorate, having served the United Methodist church in Summerville the previous

Dean Peele with Dr. Ariail.

year. Professor Crum went on to chair the Department of Religious Education, overseeing its enlargement in the coming years.

The passing of Dr. A.N. Brunson in 1936 brought grief and a sense of great loss both personally and officially to every member of the college family at Columbia College.

Professor Mason Crum

Dr. Brunson was officially connected with Columbia College longer than any other man in the history of the institution; for over 35 years he was a member of the Board of Trustees. During that time he served as Secretary, President, and during the last year of his life, President-Emeritus. During his long term of office he missed only one meeting, and never missed a commencement during 35 years. Commenting on the loss to the school, President Guilds wrote: "The value of his service to Columbia College can be calculated by no arithmetic of this earth. It is a wonderful thing for an institution to have such an official and such a friend."[14]

DURING THE WAR EFFORT[15]

Columbia College students eagerly responded to the call of national defense. Besides attending their regular classes and participating in extra-curricular activities, they

---

14   J. Caldwell Guilds, *Southern Christian Advocate*, August 31, 1939.
15   Sources for this section include: *Southern Christian Advocate*, April 30, 1942; *The Columbian*, 1942.

met Red Cross classes in first aid, home nursing, and nutrition, sometimes as frequently as three times a week. The entire college organized for possible air raids. Twelve members of the faculty were trained as air raid wardens, and student assistants were appointed to help them. The buildings were inspected for the most suitable places to take shelter. Several faculty members were certified as teachers of defense courses; the head of the Home Economics department sponsored a weekly radio program which included suggestions on intelligently buying foods for a balanced diet and helpful hints to those families buying food on a limited budget.

The 1943 Senior Class lowering the flag.

The social calendar reflected that students made 15 trips in a single month to Fort Jackson and USO centers. They performed entertaining programs by the college choir and the college dramatic department. The officials at the Fort sent for the girls in military cars, under the supervision of a chaplain; sometimes the girls invited friends from the Fort for dinner or for a program planned and presented for the boys in uniform, and every night troops were seen in the parlors and recreation hall being entertained by "special" friends.

President Guilds sent the following message to the student body during the war:

What word shall your President send you when there is so much he would like to say and little that can be said?

The world is locked in the greatest conflict of history—a conflict that will determine the destiny of all nations and all peoples of the earth. As you face this situation and as we all struggle for victory, the one word I would say to you is: See that there is no blackout in your personal development.

The world has ever looked to her women for life's ideals. When peace comes, America and the world will need, as never before, women of culture, vision, ideals, and consecration. You—the college bred women of America—will largely determine the pattern of the years ahead. See that you have to offer the best of which you are capable—in body, in mind, in spirit.

Let there be no blackout in any sphere of your personality.

CHAPTER 6—THREATS WITHIN & WITHOUT

The years following the second World War brought new challenges to the Columbia College campus. Men—mainly former GIs who could not find space in the swelling student bodies of other schools—were accepted to the college as day students. A movement within the Methodist Conference to merge the college with two others arose. Long-time President J.C. Guilds resigned, a new president taking his place (alongside a new Board of Trustees).

A PROPOSED MERGER

With little warning, conference leaders began steps toward a merger of Columbia College, along with Lander College, with Wofford in November 1947. This came by way of a joint commission for the conference, formed in 1946 to study the colleges, which presented its recommendations at a special session that same year of the two South Carolina Methodist Conferences. The proposed plan would have consolidated the three schools into one co-educational institution on a new campus (site to be selected later), and that the colleges remain as they were until all legal questions could be settled.

The proposed resolution became the battleground in the adjourned session of the Conference, and in October 1947, the "Great Debate" followed. Dr. J.O. Smith, at that point Bishop Smith, offered as a substitute to the resolution "that Methodism in South Carolina shall have one accredited college; that it be co-educational, and that it be placed on the Wofford campus. Also that two dormitories... be placed in the campus and named Columbia and Lander, respectively." This motion was rejected by a majority vote, but the resolution of the Joint College Commission, placing Columbia and Wofford under one Board of Trustees was passed on November 18, 1947.

Those closest to the college, including President J.C. Guilds and James Milton

Ariail, harbored concerns about the ultimate impact of this action on the future of an autonomous Columbia College. Alumnae and friends of the college began an active lobbying effort to have the merger decision reversed. Columbia College suffered during this perplexing period in its history—enrollments dropped from 256 in 1948 to 187 in 1951; faculty morale declined, with two faculty members accused of disloyalty; and college resources were sold. The new administration leadership also demolished the 500-seat amphitheatre, which had been erected by the Alumnae Association in 1933 after a four-year fundraising drive. The action of the uniting of Columbia and Wofford became the subject of conversations throughout the state. As the Conference of 1948 approached, speculations arose; all sorts of false rumors were rife; there was unrest in the college, and some women of the faculty spent considerable time with the Conference of 1948, advising the ministers on what they should do about Columbia College.

In the meantime friends of the college began to raise questions: Why, in May 1947, did the Conference propose moving Columbia, completely subordinating it to Wofford, and ultimately putting an end to an institution which at that time had a full enrollment, and could show evidence of progress? It appeared that some strong influence was being exerted upon the Conference; the targeting of the endowment of Columbia along with the possibility of selling its plant, as well as the idea of a possible Methodist University at Spartanburg, midway between Emory and Duke, was suspected.

Wiser heads prevailed in late 1950, when conference leaders decided to separate the institutions and establish a new Board of Trustees for Columbia College. After a brief discussion of the motion of the Rev. H.A. Whitten, the resolution to separate was adopted by a vote of 214. Thus the Conference rescinded its actions of 1947–48, and Columbia College was restored to its status prior to 1947.

A NEW PRESIDENT AND NEW LEADERSHIP ON CAMPUS[16]

Dr. Walter K. Greene

From the beginning of the movement in 1947 to unite the colleges, Dr. Guilds was strongly opposed to it. He saw that the union was not feasible, and ultimately it would mean the abolishment of Columbia College from the field of the education for women for which it was founded. When the new board was elected in October 1948, Dr. Guilds presented his resignation to the retiring Board of Trustees of Columbia College after a tenure of 27 years.

Dr. Walter K. Greene was eminently equipped for the presidency of any college when he assumed the position at the uniting of

16   Source: James M. Ariail, *A History of Columbia College*, pp. 19–24.

Columbia and Wofford. He was a scholar, experienced in the field of education, and a leader in the SC Conference. He was an attractive personality, of a pleasing appearance, and gifted with the capacity for warm friendship. He had taught at Wesleyan and came from the faculty of Duke as president of Wofford, and was the choice of the new Board to guide the united colleges.

Undoubtedly, the majority of the Conference that voted to place the two colleges under one President and one Board of Trustees sincerely believed that it would bring about a new day for Methodist education. Probably, Dr. Greene, familiar with the size of Duke, felt the same way.

On August 1, 1949, Dr. Oscar E. Lever was appointed Dean of Columbia College. He had been a teacher in the Hyatt Park School, Eau Claire, and a minister who had served churches in the state. His association with Dr. Greene began at Duke and he was closely associated with him at Wofford; from the time of his appointment as dean, he was largely responsible for the affairs of Columbia. He had come at a time when the burden was heavy and his lack of administrative experience added to his problems. Nevertheless, he undertook his responsibilities with confidence and vigor.

In recording briefly the events of the Greene administration, it must be stated that uniting the two colleges under one head, with Dr. Greene as president, created for him a situation that was neither feasible nor practical. In the time that he served, he spent many hours working over the problems of Columbia College, and if he had a longer tenure, the college likely would have prospered under his leadership. Nevertheless, there is some evidence that he never acquired full faith in the future of the college. He stopped plans for a building on campus, and ordered the plowing under of an amphitheatre which had been given by alumnae and friends. He sold property that had been given to the college for future use, for much less than the former board had valued it. He also cancelled the agreement with the Pearce-Young-Angel Wholesale Company; in 1947, the trustees had entered into an agreement with this established firm in Columbia, the terms of which were that the college should erect a facility which the company would use, pay all taxes, and in 20 years the college would own the property and the firm would pay rent. Had the contract been carried out, the college would have owned a property later to be valued at a much higher figure than the original investment.

Dr. Greene's report on Columbia College given to the SC Conference of 1950 was gloomy. He stated that two of the grave problems of the college were its location and the increase in co-education in the University, and the four competitive colleges for women in the state which seemed to have more complete educational plans and instructional facilities than Columbia. He attributed the decrease in the number of students to its lack of an adequate library, a science building, and a gymnasium. The student enrollment of 1948–49 was 256; in 1949–50 it was 236; and for 1951 it was hoped the enrollment would be 200. As a matter of record the enrollment for 1951–52 was 187, with 40 applications reported.

Following the vote to re-separate the colleges in 1950, Columbia College moved on academically—largely because of its able faculty. However, there was evidence of decline in morale.

CHAPTER 7 — A NEW DAWN FOR WOMEN'S EDUCATION

I n February 1951, Columbia College's future as a viable institution for women's higher education was, at best, questionable. Although loyal alumnae and friends of the college had successfully convinced Methodist Conference leaders to rescind the merger with Wofford College, the newly reconstituted Board of Trustees confronted formidable challenges. Student enrollment had dwindled to a mere 151 students, the endowment stood at a bleak $350,000, and the ability to make monthly payroll for the ensuing year was uncertain. Numerous conference leaders, including Bishop Costen J. Harrell and even some of the college trustees, harbored doubts about the college's ability to survive.

ANOTHER NEW PRESIDENT

Members of the Board of Trustees knew that the selection of the institution's next president would be a critical factor in the college's future. As the Board considered its responsibilities and options, the name of an articulate and energetic young minister surfaced—R. Wright Spears. The 38-year-old minister of Central Methodist Church in Florence, Spears was a South Carolina native, a graduate of Wofford College, and held a Bachelor of Divinity from Duke University. In March 1951 the trustees tapped him to become Columbia College's

Inauguration of President R. Wright Spears (kneeling) in 1951. Pictured with Reverend Melvin Medlock (left) and Bishop Casten J. Harrell (center).

twelfth president. Under his leadership the college launched a rebuilding program that shaped and defined the institution's character for the next half-century.

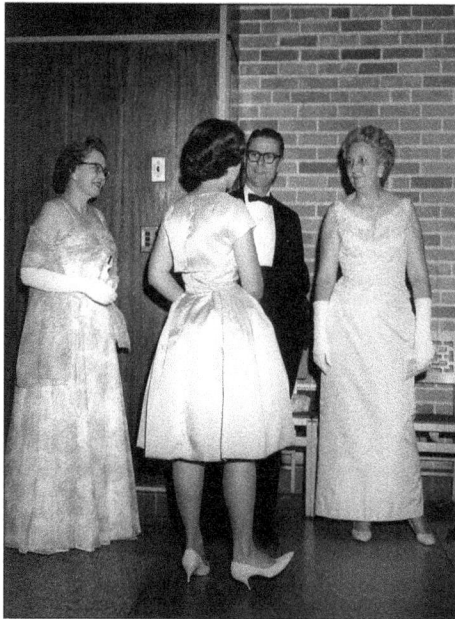

Miss Anne Clements, Dean of Women, with President and Mrs. Spears at a student reception.

The young president enthusiastically embraced the challenges confronting Columbia College. His first step was to secure loans that enabled the college to meet payrolls. An inspiring and effective communicator, Spears then canvassed the state to meet with prospective students and their parents to personally provide information on the special Columbia College experience. He recruited new faculty and administrators, including Thomas G. Shuler, who was appointed Assistant to the President and Academic Dean. Throughout the first year President Spears met with alumnae, community and business leaders and church and lay leaders to project confidence and commitment to Columbia College's mission in women's higher education. By the end of the year he had pulled off a major fundraising feat with the conference's decision to contribute the widely sought $160,000 Lander Fund to Columbia College, despite the Bishop's public description of the college as a "sinking ship."

Over the next five years, Spears' capable and enthusiastic leadership style restored confidence and secured a firm foundation for the institution and its mission. Between 1951 and 1956 new buildings were erected: Fleming Hall (the current Allison Administration Building), the Student Center, and Gonzales Hall (the site of the new Student Union). In addition, new activities that today are regarded as Columbia College "traditions" were introduced, including Ludy Bowl (1955) and Senior Communion at commencement.

In 1977 President Spears announced plans for retirement. His 26-year term left a deep footprint on the institution clearly evident in campus structures: Fleming, Gonzales, Wesley, Hudson, and Asbury Dormitories; T.J. Harrelson Student Center; Ariail Peele Academic Building; the President's House; Cottingham Theater; Reeves Science Building; Daniel Dining Hall; J. Drake Edens Library; and Godbold Physical Education Center. His imprint on the institution extended through the outstanding faculty and staff he recruited who became part of the Columbia College experience for generations of students. And the Spears legacy was indelibly reflected in the lives of the thousands of students who participated in the life of Columbia College during his quarter century of leadership and took a piece of that experience with them as they entered the rapidly changing world of late 20th-century America.

CENTENNIAL CELEBRATION

In 1954 Columbia College had much to celebrate as it entered its centennial year. The college family of alumnae, faculty, staff, trustees, students and loyal friends joined hands to organize a spectacular Centennial Celebration that provided monthly special events to highlight the college's heritage and included an historical pageant, "The Columbia College Story," written and produced by faculty member and Columbia College graduate Anne Frierson Griffin. Over a hundred Columbia College students, faculty, and staff participated in the highly-acclaimed pageant, which, as Dr. Spears recalled, "Gave an account of the college's encounter with tragedy time after time, always rising to triumph over disaster."[17]

On November 5, 1954, a time capsule, containing a range of materials on the college, was buried on East campus with the stipulation that it was to be opened by the college community in 2054. The capsule included outfits from the era (purchased by four representatives of the President's Club at Belk's Department Store); a program of the Centennial Pageant; a *Post Script*, *Criterion*, and a copy of the 1953–54 *Columbian*; a rat cap, a gym suit, a block C, a college pennant, and stickers. Also, a typical report card, a class schedule card, a date card and a week-end card, a file card, a penalty slip, a student handbook, and an academic handbook. Also a college catalogue, folders of activities of the college, a student body roll, letters from Dr. Spears and Mr. Shuler concerning the expansion program of the college, a sophomore literature book, copies of various chapel programs, a football program, a dance program, a program of the 1954 choir tour, an SCA calendar,

The 1957 Columbia College Board of Trustees (left to right): Mr. R.H. Smith, West Columbia; Mr. T.J. Harrelson, Columbia; Rev. Herbert L. Spell, Columbia; Mrs. John A. Henry, Greenville; Mrs. R.C. Gray, Columbia; Rev. Paul McWhirter, Georgetown; Mr. John E. Edens, Chairman, of Columbia; Rev. E.S. Jones, Secretary, of Columbia; Rev. J.H. Kohler, Greenville; Col. Roy C. Moore, Cheraw; Rev. D.W. Reese, Holly Hill; Rev. George Cannon, Clemson, and Mr. W.F. Bynum, Sumter. Not present for the picture were Dr. M.K. Medlock, Florence, and Mr. A.D. Cannon, Fountain Inn.

17 R. Wright Spears, *One in the Spirit*, pp. 79-80.

and a copy of 'Portals of Hope.' Also a letter from Jane Anne's 'Luke,' a picture of the 1954 President's Club to the President's Club of 2054.[18]

STRENGTHENING THE COLLEGE

Academic Dean Thomas Shuler worked closely with President Spears to build and strengthen the academic curriculum. The library was remodeled and expanded in 1952. Shuler proposed the creation of a new honorary society in 1953, The Order of the Purple Seal, to recognize excellence in student academic achievement. A local chapter of the American Association of University Professors (AAUP) was established in the late 1950s, and college officials agreed to adhere to the AAUP standards and guidelines for faculty governance. New academic offerings were added in business and speech, and a successful evening division was opened. Shuler encouraged faculty scholarship with the creation of a new campus publication, aptly titled *SEARCH*. In 1963, the college instituted a cutting edge organizational plan for student learning, the Trimester Plan, dividing the school year into three units, rather than the traditional two semesters.

Standing left to right, Dr. R. Wright Spears, President; Janet Alexander (Cotter), Alumnae Secretary; Ruth Henry Lightsey, Registrar; Dr. Thomas Shuler, Dean of Students. Seated Alumnae: Jackie Spann Hewitt (class of 1939); Eva Crosby Covington (class of 1925), Myrtle Higginbotham Groeschal (class of 1925).

The dawn of the 1960s, best represented nationally by the election of the optimistic new President John F. Kennedy, promised great new chapters in the Columbia College experience. The building program continued with the erection of the Ariail-Peele Academic Building, Kingswood Hall Dormitory (now Hudson), and the new President's Home (now Maxwell House) on Columbia College Drive in 1957. Cottingham Theater opened in 1960 and the Reeves Science Building in 1962.

As the college regained its footing, the personal touch of the administration was evident in many areas, not least in new student recruitment. Dean Shuler's devotion to the college, his tireless labor to advance the goal of "Quality Education," and his attention to detail were wed to his capacity for personal engagement with students and others. Quickly recovering from the struggles a decade before, the college swelled to record enrollment in 1960 with 647 students. Janet Alexander Cotter (class of 1956) recalled:

I remember the first time I ever saw Dean Shuler: My Mother, who is an alumna, brought me, green and scared, to see the college of my choice and to ask the Dean if there might be just the slightest possibility of my staying in her old room in upstairs East. Tom Shuler met us with the

18 *The Post Script*, October 1954.

friendliest handshake, took us to see Mother's old room and assured me that I could stay there my freshman year. (It was not until several years later, that I realized that I could have had my choice of several dozen rooms—so small was the student body!) But Tom met us with warmth and personal interest; and we felt it.

It has been like this with Tom—he is vitally interested in every student at C.C.; and they know it. Who else in this world could stand at the front door as freshmen are arriving at the college, shake each girl's hand and call her by name?

Thomas Shuler's worth to Columbia College is immeasurable. When Columbia College honored Dean Shuler with the prestigious Medallion, she recognized excellence and loyalty at their finest.[19]

ANOTHER DEVASTATING FIRE

A tragic fire jolted the campus in the early morning hours of February 12, 1964. Slumbering students, accustomed to routine fire drills, responded to the real life drama playing out before them, quickly exiting their dormitories and tearfully huddling in pajamas and bathrobes in College Place Church. There President Spears reminded them that not a single life had been lost and that "nothing has been destroyed that cannot be rebuilt." The campus fire destroyed the college's East Dormitory and gutted its landmark structure, Old Main (where today's Breed leadership now stands.) As the sun rose in the hours following the fire, the stately columns of Old Main remained as a visible reminder of the spirit of Columbia College. In the months and years ahead, "the Columns" became the Columbia College symbol, the title of its alumnae publication, and ultimately would be incorporated into her logo.

The fire took a heavy toll on the college, with the music, art, and business departments

The East Wing Dormitory of Old Main burning on February 11, Ash Wednesday, 1964.

---

19 Janet Alexander Cotter (class of 1956) in *Columbia College Magazine*, Summer 1967.

destroyed. In a single night faculty members lost notes, records and research that were emblems of professional academic life. Business department chairman Cecil Bierley lost the only copy of the manuscript for his nearly completed doctoral dissertation. The $40,000 pipe organ, numerous pianos and paintings went up in flames. Almost a third of the student body lost all their personal possessions. Damage was estimated at $2 million, with only $750,000 covered in insurance. Bob Barham, college treasurer, worked tirelessly with the insurance companies and college leaders. He and Dean Shuler made sure that the students had dormitory rooms and that classes resumed within 48 hours.

College officials immediately launched fundraising efforts to rebuild the campus. In this effort, Trustee Chairman T.J. Harrelson and Alumnae Association President Alawee Gibson Tucker, class of 1939, assumed key leadership roles and worked closely with President Spears. Fundraising drives netted $2 million. Alawee Tucker accepted the unprecedented challenge of raising $100,000 from alumnae and canvassed the state with young alumnae director MaryAnn Smith Eubanks Crews. Their untiring efforts led to results that widely exceeded the goal with over $370,000 raised, the 2005 equivalent of well over $2 million dollars. The impact on campus was immediate: Eighteen months after the fire, three new dormitories —Wesley, Hudson, and Asbury—were opened, the dining hall remodeled and a classroom wing added to Cottingham Theater. Enrollment soared to an all-time high of 821 students.

Reenactment of safely evacuated students gathered in College Place Methodist Church, following the 3:00 a.m. devastating campus fire of February 11, 1964. President Spears led the student body in a prayer of thanksgiving after determining there had been no injuries.

PART II:
PROMINENT FACES
& PLACES

CHAPTER 8—COLLEGE PLACES

Many campus buildings and structures have come to be iconic in the minds of alumnae and friends of the college, both because of the events and activities held there and for the people in whose honor and/or memory they have been erected.

VERA YOUNG THOMAS MEMORIAL LIBRARY (NOW JANET ALEXANDER COTTER ALUMNAE HALL)

May 30, 1953, marked the formal opening of the long-awaited addition to the Vera Young Thomas Memorial Library at Columbia College. A completely remodeled modern building now stood where once Mrs. V.M. Salley, librarian, and her staff worked patiently in restricted quarters to meet the demands of a rapidly growing student body. The building, which once consisted of a reading room and a stack section, contained a librarian's office, main reading room, reference room, audio-visual room, two classrooms, a stack section, and a spacious section for magazines upstairs, as well as a number of closets and additional storage space.

The main reading room was furnished with blonde birch furniture including round and rectangular apronless and occasional tables. Sectional sofas, arm chairs, and reading chairs upholstered in coral, yellow, light and dark green leather, offered a pleasant contrast with the light green walls and blending drapes. An attractive magazine display lines one wall; nearby easy chairs and low tables invite comfortable reading. Huge brick fireplaces at either end added a touch of warmth and dignity to the gay and inviting room. Two large blonde birch card catalog cabinets occupied one wall while opposite is a modern atlas and dictionary stand.

COTTINGHAM THEATRE

Cottingham Theatre

With dignity and charm Cora Stackhouse graced the campus of Columbia Female College during her student years, 1891 through 1895. She used the training she received here, coupled with her native abilities, to become an outstanding public school teacher in South Carolina. She married Dr. W.J. Cottingham, a dentist, and moved to Collman, Alabama. After her husband's death she returned to her family home in Latta, where she lived until her death in 1958. Her love for Columbia College and her interest in Christian higher education were displayed in her bequest, naming the college residuary legatee of her estate. The legacy represented the largest gift to the Methodist educational institution in South Carolina, according to President R. Wright Spears.

The Cottingham Theatre, located on the southwest corner of the campus, was completed in 1960. Its seating capacity is 376. The building included a standing foyer, the theatre proper, a projection and lighting room, a stagecraft room, a costume room, four classrooms, faculty offices, etc.[20]

HARRELSON STUDENT CENTER

Columbia College students danced in the New Student Center for the first time on a Saturday night in 1962, finding the facility to be as modern as the new popular dance.

20 *Columbia College Magazine*, January 1961.

Generous benefactor and Trustee, T.J. Harrelson, second from left, at the Harrelson Student Center groundbreaking in 1961. The building visible on the right is the education building of College Place UMC.

Recognizing the urgent need for expansion, Upshur and Riley, Columbia architects, planned for the old student center to be completely renovated and a two-story addition attached. Lafaye-Tarrant Construction Company, also of Columbia, spent much of 1961 making this plan a reality. Terry Rowe of Columbia Office Supply Company completed the interior design and decoration.

At the time of its opening, the building housed the alumnae and development offices, guidance center, student publication offices, student activity offices, day students' lounge canteen, book store, post office, and a student lounge with adjoining patio.[21]

REEVES SCIENCE CENTER

At the rear of the Columbia College campus on the corner of Morgan Street and Burke Avenue, an imposing two-story brick structure opened in 1963. The emblem on the surface wall of the building announced its identity: science. The emblem, an atom, and an indoor pendulum clock were gifts to the college from the Class of 1962.

Architects for the building were LaFaye, Fair, LaFaye and Associates. One partner of the Columbia architectural firm was R.S. Lafaye, husband of Nell Murray, Class of 1924. Construction of the science building began following the groundbreaking ceremonies in November 1961. The contractor, McCrory Construction Company, completed the building in the fall of 1962, and the formal opening was held during Homecoming in October.

The building contained three laboratories for general biology, bacteriology and anatomy, three laboratories for chemistry, and a physics laboratory. Each of the laboratories had an adjoining storage and preparation area. There was also a large lecture-

Mrs. Reeves at left and Mr. J.M. Reeves at right of New York City stand before the Reeves Science Center in 1965.

21 *Columbia College Magazine,* January 1962.

demonstration room, a seminar room, classrooms and faculty offices on each floor.

Students in one of the new science labs study general biology in 1963.

At that time, 12 hours of sciences were required of each student for a degree from Columbia College. These requirements were satisfied through a choice of biology, chemistry, physics, mathematics and/or physical science. Major courses of study in the Science Department included general science, biology, chemistry, and mathematics.[22]

GODBOLD PHYSICAL EDUCATION CENTER

The formal consecration service for Godbold Physical Education Center was held at 3:30, Wednesday, April 21, 1972. Bishop Paul Hardin, Jr. performed the consecration service for the building, with W.J. Colvin, Jr., Chairman of the Board of Trustees, presiding over the ceremony. Dr. Warren Giese, Chairman of the Physical Education Department at USC, was guest speaker for the consecration.

The new physical education complex was named Godbold Center in honor of Miss Lucile Ellerbe Godbold. The gymnasium part of the Center was named Porter Gymnasium in memory of Mrs. Julia Inabinet Porter. The swimming pool and surrounding facilities was named the Greer Natatorium in honor of Jacque Greer, a Columbia College student.[23]

Swimming competition at Godbold Center's Greer Natatorium.

THE COLUMNS

Harkening back to the charred columns that remained standing, stretching heavenward among the ashes of the 1964 fire—a haunting yet stalwart symbol of the persevering spirit of the school—the columns have become iconic in the Columbia College community.

"As long as they stand," a senior said as she surveyed the blackened remnants of the Main Building, "Columbia College will stand. It looks like something out of ancient

---

22 *Columbia College Magazine*, March 1963.
23 *The Post Script*, April, 1972.

Rome. Columbia College will rise again. You just wait and see."[24]

Those words proved prescient as the city and state rallied alongside the college community to ensure the rebuilding of the campus. The indomitable spirit of Columbia College has, time and again, overcome tragedy and challenge; not least in the face of greatest catastrophe to strike. Instead of a sign of defeat, the columns have become an icon of endurance, just as "the columns will rise again" became the mantra of many and a constant reminder from MaryAnn Smith Eubanks Crews, then alumnae director.

They are nearly omnipresent: echoed in the architecture of the Johnny Cordell Breed Leadership Center for Women and elsewhere throughout campus; in the title of the alumnae magazine; on logos, websites, and printed materials. Most of all, in the memorial structure, "The Columns Gazebo," erected through the generosity of Alawee Gibson Tucker in honor of all who rallied alongside the college during its time of need.

As the editors of *The State* newspaper observed in the days following the fire: from the crackling flames and the smoldering ashes of the college's tragedy, some truths about the institution, its students, faculty, administrative staff, alumnae and the community emerged. The truths are those of the spirit.

- Columbia College was and is, in the well-chosen word of senior English Prof. J. Milton Ariail, "indestructible." Both the professor and the senior student were right in that the college "will rise again. You just wait and see." Within weeks, the trustees of the college began plans for rebuilding.

- The value of the college to the Columbia and Carolina community was reinforced. The city and the state required in those times, as they do today, the distinctive education imparted by the small denominational school—secure and honest in intellectual, moral, and spiritual knowledge. Symbolic was the prayer session, thanking God for the physical safety of the student body, held by President Wright Spears and the young ladies the morning of the tragic fire.

- The qualities of character that typify the endurance of Carolinians and Columbians rose swiftly to the surface. The young ladies of the college displayed their presence of mind and a singular courage in their orderly evacuation of their dormitories. Firemen risked their lives, venturing perilously close to tumbling walls, in a lost cause. Citizens of the area rose from their beds to offer their services—preparing a hot breakfast for the girls, opening the doors to their homes in supernumerary compassion. In all, Carolinians and Columbians evidenced a 'gentilesse' that has been characteristic of the state's people in the past.[25]

These truths and more are embodied in the Columns. "She who has been, shall ever be; wise, good, and true eternally." Long may they stand!

---

24 Editorial, *The Columbia Record*, February 14, 1964.
25 *Ibid*.

CHAPTER 9—AFTER THE FIRE

Amazingly, campus life moved on after the fire of 1964, with staff and faculty pressing forward in characteristic Columbia College perseverance. The stability of the faculty and other prominent and beloved members of the college community contributed greatly to the enduring spirit, as did the tireless efforts of those whose commitment to the college saw its re-building through. Nevertheless, cultural changes and influences found their way onto the Columbia College campus, causing new challenges in addition to the progress they brought.

ACTIVISM AND SOCIAL CHANGES ON CAMPUS

The dramatic social and cultural changes that swept the country during the 1960s were clearly felt on the Columbia College campus. A racial moderate, President Spears actively engaged in and helped shape community efforts to end segregation and facilitate a transition to integration. The college published its compliance with the Civil Rights Act of 1964 in its 1965 college catalogue. Although black students attended special summer programs in 1965, Lillian Irene "Bunny" Woods became the college's first African American enrolled as a matriculating student in September 1966. Strong ties to the United Methodist Conference undoubtedly resulted in interest from black Methodists in having their daughters attend Columbia College. By 1977, African American students comprised 16 percent of the student enrollment. The Board of Trustees welcomed its first black member, the Reverend Omega Newman, who served from 1974–1978.

Lillian Irene "Bunny" Woods sings with the Columbia College Choir in 1967.

The strong and determined leadership that resulted in so many dynamic changes on campus did not go unchallenged in all matters. In the late 1960s, a small number of young faculty questioned what they perceived as an autocratic leadership style by key college officials. Faculty activists voiced strong concerns about administrative decisions on contract renewals and were particularly concerned when the contracts of non-tenured faculty were not renewed. Faculty members tested the limits of academic freedom in 1968 by frequenting an anti-Vietnam War coffeehouse on Columbia's Main Street. In a highly controversial trial that concerned the closing of the coffeehouse as a public "nuisance," two Columbia College faculty members—one tenured and one non-tenured—were called to testify about their visits to the coffeehouse. When the administration subsequently decided not to renew the non-tenured faculty member's contract, critical faculty voices questioned the understanding of academic freedom by the campus leadership.

Gloria Grainger (class of 1969), the first black graduate with the Columbia College Dance Company in the 1969 Columbian.

A number of Columbia College students, inspired by the emerging youth movement and the highly visible new women's movement, began to demand greater freedoms in their lives on campus. Students entering the college as freshmen as late as the fall of 1968 complained that they were expected to follow regulations that had been in place during their mothers' generation. Articles in *The Postscript* complained about overly parental supervision by college officials and openly questioned the wisdom of the college's restrictive rules, especially the strict limitations on off campus visiting hours and the dress code, in preparing them for independent living after graduation. In 1970, new student governance policies were implemented that removed curfews for upperclassmen and relaxed the dress code. In a particularly activist moment, several students participated in a campus "march" on the president's home in 1970 to protest the administration's failure to renew the contracts of several popular faculty members.

The movement for equal rights and expanded opportunities for women gained considerable following and support among Columbia College students of the late 1960s and early 70s. Women faculty members provided important models for student leadership and achievement. An increasing number of women joined the college's faculty and assumed chairmanships of academic departments. Moreover, in the early 1970s, two important events occurred that marked the clear emergence of new roles for women on campus: the election of Clelia Derrick Hendrix, Class of 1941, as the first woman to chair the college's Board of Trustees and the appointment of Dr. Ann

Flowers as the college's Academic Dean, the first woman to serve in the key academic post.

OTHER PROMINENT FIGURES ON CAMPUS

VON ETTA MILHOUS SALLEY

Mrs. Salley's name was almost synonymous with the library at Columbia College during the 1930s, 40s and 50s. She was *the* librarian from 1930–1963 and continued as professor of Library Science until 1966.

In order to become fully accredited by the Southern Association of Colleges and Schools the college needed, among other requirements, a librarian with a degree from a library school. Mrs. Salley was working at USC and going to Columbia University during the summer months to receive her master's there. Dr. Guilds, then president of Columbia College, went to USC and offered her the position.

Von Etta Milhous Salley

Mrs. Salley received her master's degree and the library grew. She credited Dr. Ariail with helping greatly in the selection of materials, and she was grateful to the Alumnae Association for drives to raise money and for donating books. On April 1, 1938, Dr. Guilds telegraphed the news from Dallas, Texas, that Columbia College had been admitted to the Southern Association of Colleges as a standard senior college.

There were only a few annual reports that Mrs. Salley made, but she left indelible marks in the hearts of many students.[26]

LUCILE ELLERBE GODBOLD (MISS LUDY)

From 1922 to 1980—over 58 years—Lucile Ellerbe Godbold was a fixture on the Columbia College campus. The daughter of a Columbia College alumna, Godbold was a 1922 graduate of Winthrop College. In that same year she gained national and international fame as she won six medals, including a gold medal in shot put that set a new world record, at the first women's Olympic competition in Paris. Upon her return to South Carolina a crowd of over 1500 welcomed her in her hometown of Estill, including then Governor and Mrs. Wilson G. Harvey. Fifty years later in 1972, Estill commemorated her accomplishments with an historic marker.

Lucile Ellerbe Godbold

Godbold joined the Columbia College faculty in the fall of 1922

---

26 This account of Mrs. Salley was given by Elizabeth "Tootsie" DuRant (class of 1950).

and over the next half-century became South Carolina's preeminent champion for women's athletics. Known affectionately as "Miss Ludy," she directed the college's physical education department and under her tutelage young women learned the fundamentals of basketball, hockey, tennis, and other field sports as well as the important lessons of team building. The college's annual intramural athletic competition, Ludy Bowl, carries her name.

"American girl athletes who will represent the United States in the international athletic contests to start in the Pershing Stadium at Paris, August 30, are seen in this group." The Cincinnati Enquirer, Sunday, August 20, 1922. Lucile E. Godbold is the first person standing on the left. Kneeling: Maybelle Gilliland, Elizabeth Stine, Captain Frolieda Batson, Janet Snow, Camille Sable. Standing: Lucile Ellerbe Godbold, France Meade, Nancy Voorhees, Suzanne Becker, Lousie Voorhes, Anna Hardwick, Esther Greene.

By the 1960s Miss Ludy had become a legendary figure on campus and virtually every Columbia College student of her era could recall the first campus contact with her. Godbold oversaw the campus fire drill program and her precise, efficient manner was largely responsible for the remarkable student exit from the dormitories in the early morning hours of the 1964 fire. Known for her wit and humor, she delighted students and faculty alike with her flamboyant portrayal of "Flaming Mamie" in the yearly Faculty Follies. When the college's new athletic complex opened in 1971, it was named in her honor. The college awarded her its highest honor in 1980 when she was one of the initial group of five who became Columbia College's first Medallion recipients.

Miss Ludy's professional accomplishments place her at the forefront of women's achievement in South Carolina and mark her as a key participant in South Carolina's women's history. In 1961 she was elected the first woman to the South Carolina Athletic Hall of Fame. In 2005 she was inducted posthumously into the South Carolina Hall of Fame.

The First Ludy Bowl, Saturday November 19, 1955, with the Gonzales Gorillas claiming victory over the Humphries Honeys.

MR. GUTHRIE DARR

Guthrie Darr was born in Pocono Manor, Pennsylvania, the son of a Congregational minister. A graduate of Pomona College in Claremont, California, Darr received an M.A. degree in musicology from the Claremont Graduate School. Darr arrived at Columbia College in the fall of 1949 where he quickly entered the hearts of all who knew him. In addition to teaching Music Theory, Music Appreciation, Music History, Form and Analysis and Conducting, he directed the Columbia College Choir and the

Choral Club. He began the small choral group known as the High C's. He also directed the Chancel Choir at Shandon United Methodist Church and the Columbia Choral Society.

For many years, he was "Mr. Music" at Columbia College, at Shandon United Methodist Church, and in the city of Columbia. Not only did he have tremendous musical talent and was able to get unbelievable sounds from those groups he worked with, he had a warm and loving personality and was loved by all who knew him. Mr. Darr retired from Columbia College in 1993 and from all musical groups in 1998. He was awarded the Columbia College Medallion in 1993 and the Elizabeth O'Neill Verner Award in 1982.

Guthrie Darr conducts choir rehearsal.

Columbia College will always remember Guthrie and his wonderful contributions to the college and to the women he helped become the musicians they are who continue to help "Sing the Praise of Her We Love." Mr. Darr died in 2012.[27]

Robert T. "Bob" Barham

President Spears contacted Bob Barham in December of 1957, offering him the position of Director of Public Relations. Barham accepted and began work for the college in March 1958. His duties included student recruitment, managing the Placement Office

Left to right, Helen Jeffords Barham, Robert T. "Bob" Barham, Arlene Shuler, Dean Thomas Shuler, Mary Blue Spears, President R. Wright Spears and other faculty and staff greet students in 1970 for a formal reception.

and the Business Office staff, overseeing the News Service, bringing special groups to the campus, attending special events, and many others including, as Bob said, "Doing whatever else President Spears and Dean Shuler wanted me to do!"

On February 12, 1964, his duties increased tremendously when the fire destroyed the center complex of the college. Bob was involved in preparation of the statement of loss and in negotiations with the insuring company. Help for the college came in the presence of an expert sent by the Methodist Church and the college's law

27 Some portions of this account taken from *Columbia College Alumnae Magazine*, May 1962.

firm. It took four years to settle the claim and the case went all the way to the SC Supreme Court.

After an illness in 1984, it was decided that Bob should leave the rigors of the Business Office. He was named the Planned Giving Officer in the college's Development Office, charged with contacting alumnae and friends of the college to seek gifts through planned giving, which he did until his retirement in 1993. Although there were many difficult times in his career at CC, there were also many happy times. Bob recalled that MaryAnn Smith (Class of 1959, now Mrs. MaryAnn Smith Eubanks Crews), Director of Alumnae Affairs, called to say they needed a piano for the parlor in Alumnae Hall. His response was, "Where do you think I'm going to get a piano?" No sooner had we completed our conversation when Bob's secretary told him a lady was waiting to talk to him on the other line, who said, "Mr. Barham, I would like to give the college a piano." Accepting her offer, he then called MaryAnn. "I have a piano for you. Is that fast enough!?"

CHAPTER 10—PREPARING LEADERS

Perhaps no theme better characterized Columbia College's mission in the last decades of the twentieth century than the college's role in nurturing women's leadership and producing women leaders. With the onset of Title IX regulations in the 1970s that required gender equity in educational programs, the college reaffirmed its commitment to women's higher education and its status as a woman's college.

AN INCREASED FOCUS ON WOMEN'S LEADERSHIP

In the last decades of the 20th century, intensive academic programs in leadership—including a new leadership minor, an impressive new women's leadership building on the college's front campus, and a new partnership with the South Carolina Commission on Women—propelled Columbia College to the forefront of efforts to tap and utilize the enormous leadership potential of women.

Although service to the greater community runs throughout the history of the college and has been a long-standing expectation for Columbia College graduates, the institution's recent leadership emphasis is grounded in historically significant and transforming experiences in women's lives. The enormous social and economic changes affecting women in the 1960s and 70s, especially in the area of women's employment, sparked new roles for women's colleges and other higher educational institutions across the country. Columbia College began a continuing education program for women, to serve the increasing number of adult women who had postponed or deferred college enrollment because of marriage and family obligations. Within a few years this program led to the development of a Women's Evening College for adult working women, with majors in business administration, social work, and public affairs. The faculty structured new academic requirements for returning women students that reflected understandings of the wide range of life experiences that these women brought to their undergraduate studies.

In the 1970s increasing numbers of traditionally aged students considered careers in professional areas long dominated by men. Always a strong advocate for women's leadership in educational careers, Columbia College now actively explored new ways to assist her students in pursuing various career options, especially in the areas of law, public policy, the arts, and the sciences. Faculty and administrators designed innovative career-oriented programs grounded in the liberal arts in business administration, speech correction, physical and health education, career writing, social work, and journalism. Virtually every academic department provided career-focused activities for its majors and many developed internship experiences that linked academic study to real work environments in the arts, business, politics, government, and media. The faculty approved a Contractual Studies major for highly motivated students who sought interdisciplinary study and designed new graduate programs in English, education and music. The college's Placement Office, largely a résumé and reference letter repository for graduates up to the 1960s, became a comprehensive life planning and career center that sponsored a wide range of career orientation services and helped retool older alumnae for personal and career transitions.

LEADERSHIP UNDER A NEW PRESIDENT[28]

After the long and faithful tenure of President Spears, in 1978 Dr. Ralph T. Mirse was appointed Columbia College's 13th president. An ordained Methodist minister and Kentucky native with degrees from the Asbury Theological Seminary and Boston University, Dr. Mirse brought new perspectives to the campus and launched impressive efforts in administrative restructuring, budgeting, continuing education, and fundraising. During his administration enrollment increased from 800 students to 1200 students. Dr. Mirse established sister-college relationships with Sungshin Women's University in South Korea and with San Buenaventura University in Colombia. First Lady Blanche Allen Mirse was an active part of his administration and a dynamic campus hostess. In 1981 she hosted over 1500 guests at the Mirse Christmas Open House reception. Dr. Mirse retired in 1988. Epworth dormitory was renamed for the couple in 1992. Mrs. Mirse was a Medallion Recipient in 1986; Dr. Mirse

President Ralph T. Mirse during his inauguration as the 13th president of Columbia College, standing with Mrs. Blanche Mirse and Dr. R. Wright Spears, 1978.

28 Some material from this segment came from *The Columbia College Record*, Fall 1977.

received a Medallion in 1997.

Dr. Mirse, a native of Carrsville, Ky., officially came to Columbia College as its 13ᵗʰ president on September 1, 1978. He earned the Bachelor of Arts degree and the Master of Divinity degree from Asbury Theological Seminary in Wilmore, Kentucky. From Boston University, he received the PhD degree. His extensive background in the field of higher education included service at Boston University in the Department of Sociology and Religion; Christian Theological School in Indianapolis; St. Paul School of Theology in Kansas City, Missouri; and Lliff School of Theology in Denver. He was vice president of Baker University in Baldwin City, Kansas, from 1970 to 1974 and president of Lakeland College in Sheboygan, Wisconsin, from 1974 until his selection as Columbia College president. Dr. Mirse was also a United Methodist minister, serving pastorates in Kentucky and Massachusetts.

President Ralph T. Mirse; 1986 standing before the Spears Music Art Center.

Shortly after his appointment, Dr. Mirse launched efforts to secure a stronger financial base and to expand the network of college supporters. Mirse actively encouraged new programs to attract and retain students and championed an international exchange program that linked Columbia College with Sungshin Women's University in South Korea. In 1984 the college enrollment reached an all time high of 1200 students including a small group of South Korean women. Mirse worked closely with alumnae leaders to ensure their understanding of college needs and created a new Board of Visitors, a Ministers Advisory Committee, and a Parents Committee. Mirse then spearheaded the college's "New Horizons Campaign," co-chaired by Governor John C. West and trustee Leon S. Goodall, which by 1986 had raised some $8.5 million.

DIVERSITY EXPANDS ON CAMPUS

In the 1980s and 1990s dramatic transformations occurred on the Columbia College campus. A more diverse student body—in age, race, religion, residency, and nationality—brought new interests and perspectives. Methodist students were outnumbered by students from other Protestant denominations for the first time in the institution's history, and the Board of Trustees included more lay members, especially women and other minorities. The need for campus diversity in students, faculty, staff, and academic programs became clear. A Diversity Committee, comprised of faculty, administrative staff, and students, was established in the 1990s. Columbia College observed the

Martin Luther King Birthday with special programs and activities that explored matters of social justice. As Columbia College experienced the last decade of the 20th century, African-Americans made important strides on campus with the election by college trustees of its first African-American Board Chair, Helen Nelson Grant, class of 1981; the election by students of its first African-American student government president, Acacia Bamberg; and the awarding of tenure to its first African-American professor, Dr. Sheila Elliott, from the History and Political Science Department.

Acacia Bamberg (class of 1995).

Supreme Court Justice Sandra Day O'Connor gave the commencement address in 1982. She is greeted by Dr. Belinda Friedman Gergel at a reception held in Alumnae Hall. Marlena Refern Lewis also pictured.

Embracing the increasing diversity in culture, especially for women and minorities, Columbia College hosted U.S. Supreme Court Justice Sandra Day O'Connor (the first woman to be appointed to the Supreme Court) as commencement speaker in 1982. In 1990, poet and author Maya Angelou visited the campus, in celebration of both Black History Month and Women's History Month.

Maya Angelou, American poet, author, historian, educator, civil-rights activist, and playwright.

ACTIVE ALUMNAE[29]

"Ultimately, alumnae are the college," said Dr. Ralph T. Mirse. "A college comes to be known in part through the success and achievements of its graduates. A college recruits a kind of student in part because of the kinds of students it has already had."

In an interview early in his tenure, Dr. Mirse placed great emphasis on the significance of the alumnae to the college—and the significance of the college to the alumnae. "There is no way to separate alumnae from their colleges," he said. "It's just one of those inevitabilities of life—once you have been part of an institution, it's a part of your life from then on."

Such automatic identifying of a person with his or her alma mater brings with it obligations on the part of the institution. Alumnae in turn, have an obligation to maintain their interest in the college, keep themselves informed about it and participate in its life and activities in whatever ways they can. "Columbia College is a

---

29 Some parts of this segment are excerpts from *Columbia College Alumnae Magazine*, Spring 1982.

very special kind of place," Dr. Mirse said. "I would think its alumnae would want to promote its interests, speak well of its program and offer financial support."

Alumnae Association Executive Committee members Anne Turner Harrell (class of 1957), MaryAnn Smith Eubanks (class of 1959), Janet Alexander Cotter (class of 1956), Lucinda Edwards Daniels (class of 1960), and Alumnae Director Edith Collins Hause (class of 1956), welcome Dr. and Mrs. Mirse at the entrance of the President's House.

The Alumnae Association celebrated its centennial in 1982, in the same place the college itself began: at Washington Street United Methodist Church. Those who gathered in the crowded church were a part of a moving service of gratitude and renewed dedication. A centennial anthem, written by then-senior Cherie Parker, was performed under the direction of Guthrie Darr. Janet Alexander Cotter, trustee and chairman of the Alumnae Centennial Committee, presented the address, "A Century of Service." An excerpt from "The Centennial Pageant" was performed by college staff and faculty, and Bishop Roy C. Clark offered the invocation. Dr. C.J. Lupo, Jr., minister of Washington Street Church, provided a message of welcome to alumnae and friends of the college. Alumnae Association President Becky Baker Pugh delivered the closing prayer.

INCREASED FACULTY INVOLVEMENT

The Columbia College faculty took decisive steps to confirm its role in academic governance and to address key issues impacting academic life on campus. Beginning with the selection of President Mirse, faculty representatives assumed active roles in Presidential Search Committees and in the selection of its chief academic leaders. Faculty governance initiatives intensified with the establishment in the 1990s of the faculty chair and vice chair positions, elected by the faculty, to oversee faculty meetings and represent faculty interests and concerns to the president, key college administrators, and the Board of Trustees. For the first time in recent memory, the faculty chair, rather than the college president or dean, presided over monthly faculty meetings. Dr. Sandra Nelson, from the college's Department of English, was elected the college's first Faculty Chair and Dr. Laurie Hopkins, from the

Dr. Sandra Nelson O'Neal of the English Department was elected to serve as the first Faculty Chair.

college's Mathematics department, served as its first vice chair.

Faculty members became advocates for new academic programs and activities. In the early 1990s women faculty recommended the creation of a Women's Studies program and took the lead in establishing a Women's Studies minor. The new program sponsored three conferences that drew national scholars to the campus. The faculty also reconsidered its general education core curriculum and added two signature courses for first year students: one exploring the role of liberal arts learning and the other the role of women in society. Faculty leadership spearheaded new emphases in women's health, athletics, the Washington Semester Program, travel study programs, and the Center for Engaged Learning to provide new ways to enhance academic learning and study.

Advances by President Mitchell

Columbia College's mission in women's higher education gained regional and national attention under the leadership of Dr. Peter T. Mitchell, appointed President in 1988. An articulate and energetic leader, Mitchell advocated a learning environment that empowered women students and infused leadership studies through all phases of the campus experience. He worked with faculty and staff to create the Collaborative Learning Center (CLC) in 1990 to facilitate dynamic faculty and student interaction. The CLC, located in the heart of the campus in Edens Library, sponsored faculty-student discussions, seminars, and research. Its weekly lunchtime discussion programs concerning current events, academic issues, and various campus concerns became an important campus forum and encouraged student- faculty interaction in dynamic new ways outside the confines of the classroom. Initiatives in Collaborative Learning were an important component of the college's selection in 1996 as a prestigious Theodore Hesburgh award recipient, one of only five colleges in the nation so recognized.

Mitchell worked closely with faculty and staff to refine the college's leadership mission. In 1990 Columbia College established The Leadership Institute to institutionalize and infuse leadership initiatives throughout the curriculum and campus. Mitchell secured funding to erect the Johnnie Cordell Breed Leadership Center for Women on the site of the Old Main building destroyed in the 1964 fire. During this period, enrollment reached 1320 students and SAT scores for incoming students improved. In 1994 *U.S. News and World Report* recognized Columbia College with a 4th place ranking as one of that year's Top Ten Liberal Arts Colleges in the South. An accomplished fundraiser, Mitchell oversaw the "Campaign for Leadership," which raised more than $17 million over a five-year period. *Synergy* and *collaboration* were Dr. Mitchell's buzzwords, and he lived them.

THE CENTENNIAL QUILT

The golden jubilee celebration of the Columbia College Alumnae Association, celebrating the 100th anniversary of the association, began in January 1982 and culminated with the unveiling of a centennial quilt. The quilt was designed to depict important factors in the life of Columbia College since its founding in 1854. The quilt squares were stitched by alumnae. The squares (from top, left to right) include:

- The Columbian—the college yearbook
- The cross—symbol of the Christian foundation of the college
- Old Main (1910–1964)—the nucleus of the campus housing administrative offices, classrooms, practice halls, the auditorium and parlors.
- Alumnae Hall—(formerly the Vera Young Thomas Memorial Library) renamed after the 1964 campus fire. This is the oldest building on the campus. Alumnae contributed funds to create parlors here.
- The Seal (*non quim sed quid*)—the Latin words translated mean "Not who but what."
- Alma Mater (first verse)—written by Dr. James Milton Ariail, Stackhouse Professor of English until his death in 1976.
- The Columns—symbols of the white columns that graced the central buildings of the old college before the fire in 1964.
- The Centennial Year—The Alumnae Association was organized on June 21, 1882, the fifth oldest in the United States.
- Edens Library—named for J. Drake Edens, trustee and benefactor. The library was constructed in 1967 and houses over 155,000 volumes.
- College Logo—depicts the lamp of learning. The two Cs (Columbia College) are the base of the lamp.
- The fountain—given by the classes of 1925, '26, '27 and '28. It graced the front campus for many years.
- Centennial Committee Members—appointed in 1980 to plan the events of the celebration.[30]

CHAPTER 10 ADDENDUM: A CENTURY OF SERVICE[31]

The War Between the States was over, and Columbia lay in ashes. Most of the buildings had been burned, but strangely enough, the college stood. And what was the reason? The college was empty now. The soldiers had been at the college gate with torches ready to burn it when a professor stopped them. He told them they must take a note <u>to Sherman, and</u> they jeered.

30 *The State*, June 19, 1982
31 History narrative given at Washington Street United Methodist Church for Columbia College Alumnae Association Centennial. January 31, 1982 by Janet Alexander Cotter (class of 1956).

'I am a Northerner, too." He said, as he wrote it.

'To General Sherman. I pray your good graces to spare Columbia College where I am a professor. I knew you in a happier occasion some years ago as a professor of music in Ohio. I taught your sister.'

Mrs. Harry T. Huffman serves tea to costumed alumnae Janet Alexander Cotter (class of 1956), Alawee Gibson Tucker (class of 1939), Edith Collins Hause (class of 1956), and Anne Turner Harrell (class of 1957) from an elite Limoges tea set that had been hand-painted by her aunt, Dovie Hyatt Lorick, in a turn-of-the-century art class at Columbia College. Lorick's father, F.H. Hyatt, donated the land on which Columbia College stands today.

And the college was saved, but it was destitute.

It was leased first as headquarters for the army, then the Catholic sisters used it as a refuge when their convent was burned, then as a hospital for wounded...and finally, as an asylum for the indigent.

All that was left were 8 pianos and a debt of $19,000.

Sherman had burned all hotels in the city and there was a manager who was glad to lease the empty college. So it prospered for 7 years as a hotel.

Had the Methodists forgotten their daughters?

The conference had learned that the Methodist Female College in Spartanburg failed. We'll never know if the conference was impressed with President Jones's ability or his assets, but he was offered the presidency of Columbia College...if he would bring his assets. What were they? Eight wagon-loads of furniture! Enough for beds in 20 rooms, chairs in most, mattresses in most.

One day in 1882, four women walked into Columbia College. They went to the parlors and found scarcely enough chairs to sit on. They went to dormitories and saw little more there. Their old classrooms had few desks, and library shelves were empty.

They were determined to do something about it, and organized "The Columbia Female College Alumnae Association," the fifth of its kind in the United States.

There was little money at that time. It took over a year, but they managed to raise $400, which went towards new furniture. And they began giving many of their personal books. In time, with assets and money, library shelves began to fill, and the grand parlor had enough chairs for young ladies and young men to sit in. Clubs were organized all over the state.

One day when I was a student at the college, the Alumnae Association President spoke to the group. The Quint Club organized.

Now Clemson had its IPTAY, but their dues were $10.00 a year, and women couldn't possibly pay that much, but they could pay $5.00 (they hoped), so this became the forerunner of the Loyalty Fund which through the years has raised thousands of dollars.

Other funds have been started – Endowment and Scholarship, and this year our goal is approximately $150,000, a little more than $400 for furniture, but given as lovingly.

Alumnae presidents always gave strong leadership, and other projects were initiated.

1964…and the college burned. This time it was not the city that lay in ashes, but it was our Columbia College.

Citizens all over the state rallied; the Governor, the city of Columbia, the mayor, the Methodist Conference, and Washington Street Church; and as always, the alumnae.

Again, they raised needed funds for beds and mattresses and desks and whatever else was necessary. They worked tirelessly.

And when the new library was built, the trustees honored the Alumnae Association with part of the old library building which became Alumnae Hall. Its parlor, the heart of the college, became the meeting place for alumnae and a welcoming place for young ladies…and their young men.

Alumnae embroidered the drapery. They shared treasured possessions – furniture, porcelains, pictures and oriental rugs.

Once again, the alumnae had a home. New programs were begun – archives, fine arts, books…

Some of us who were there stood on that fatal [sic] night in 1964, and watched the fire roar through the white columns and wondered if this would be the end. But the columns stood.

There's a small pavilion today on east campus where those columns still stand with the promise, "She who has been shall ever be…wise, good and true eternally, our own Columbia College."

CHAPTER 11—EDUCATION IN THE LATE 20TH CENTURY

A s changes in technology and education swept through the world, Columbia College leaders rose to the occasion, developing new programs and initiatives to meet educational needs. Meanwhile, alumnae and other supporters demonstrated their support for the college by providing the resources needed for building leadership among the women of CC.

EDUCATION AT THE COLLEGE

PERFORMING ARTS

Throughout its history Columbia College has been renowned for its outstanding programs in the performing arts. From the excellent string of productions at Cottingham Theatre, to the performance programs of the music department, to the choreography of the department of dance, students at the college have consistently been offered opportunities to flourish as performers in the fine arts.

COMPUTER EDUCATION

Established in the 80s, computer education courses soon became crucial for the advancement of education for women. Initially appearing at a slow pace, the

Members of Dan Wagoner and Dancers rehearse for their performance on campus

presence of the computer on campus gradually became nearly ubiquitous.

With the advent of the internet and e-mail, a computer lab was installed in the basement of the library to allow ready access for students and faculty alike.

The first computer class for faculty is conducted with new computers in the Math department.

AWARDS & RECOGNITION

The National Council for Advancement and Support of Education (CASE) announced on October 24, 1994, the selection of Dr. John Zubizarreta as the "1994 South Carolina Professor of the Year." The selection of Zubizarreta, who is a professor of English and director of the college's Honors Program, was based on his extraordinary service to students, the college, the community and the profession of teaching.[32]

U.S. News & World Report, in its "1995 Annual Guide to America's Best Colleges," rated Columbia College the fourth best regional liberal arts college in the South. To celebrate this milestone, over one thousand faculty, staff, students, alumnae, and friends of the college gathered on the Mall on September 19 to acknowledge our heritage and to look with promise toward an even more exciting future. Fifteen students, faculty, staff, and trustees, along with Bishop Joseph B. Bethea, shared the perspective that this historic event was achieved because we believed in one another, challenged one another, and cared for one another.[33]

Trustees John Redmond (spouse of Susan Hendrix Redmond, class of 1970) of Greenville and Jack Hupp (standing at podium) of Columbia celebrate with the campus in front of Edens Library.

Columbia College was one of five colleges and universities in the United States to receive a 1996 Hesburgh Award, given in honor of Rev. Theodore M. Hesburgh, president emeritus of the University of Notre Dame and a nationally renowned educator. The Hesburgh awards are given for "Faculty Development to Enhance Undergraduate Learning" and are sponsored by TIAA-CREF, the nationwide education and related non-profit financial service organization.[34]

Dr. Jerold J. Savory, professor of English and director of collaborative learning and faculty development, received the 1996 S.C. Governor's Academic Achievement Award in the Humanities. Savory was cited for "his teaching and scholarship in humanistic fields,

32 *The Columns*, Winter 1994.
33 From the *Columbia College President's Update*, Winter 1994.
34 *Columns*, Spring/Summer 1996.

THE WHITE HOUSE

WASHINGTON

February 13, 1996

Dr. Peter T. Mitchell
President
Columbia College of South Carolina
1301 Columbia College Drive
Columbia, South Carolina 29203

Dear Dr. Mitchell:

I am delighted to extend my congratulations as Columbia College receives a 1996 Hesburgh Certificate of Excellence for your collaboration for academic citizenship.

America's ability to prosper in the years to come requires a national commitment to excellence in education. Our chance to seize the opportunities before us depends on our strength of scholarship. We must build and support an educational system that offers our country's vast promise to every citizen. Only when we know that all of our students are receiving the best training possible can we truly say that we are prepared for the challenges of the future.

Innovations in teaching methods and curricula, combined with traditional lessons of ethics and good citizenship, empower our young people with a comprehensive education that will serve them well their entire lives. At Columbia, you have sought to take education beyond the boundaries of the classroom, opening new doors of opportunity and unleashing the creativity and energy of your students. I am confident that, with your leadership, the students of Columbia College can look forward to an era of great opportunity and high hopes.

Best wishes for much continued success.

Sincerely,

Bill Clinton

The February 14, 1996 letter from President Bill Clinton to Columbia College President Peter Mitchell announcing the prestigious Hesburgh Award.

particularly his commitment toward sustaining the importance of humanities in education." In addition to his recent innovative work in developing a Learning Community project which engages students and faculty in interdisciplinary study, he has published a number of books and articles on humanities topics such as community history, biography, art, literature and religion.[35]

Dr. Vivia Lawton Fowler
(class of 1976)

Dr. Vivia L. Fowler, a 1976 graduate of Columbia College, joined the faculty in 1986, serving in numerous faculty positions including chair of the Department of Religion, director of Contractual Studies, faculty chair, director of General Education, and director of the Center for Engaged Learning. Dr. Fowler was selected as Outstanding Faculty Member in 1996. In 2002 the South Carolina United Methodist Conference recognized her contributions to higher education with the Francis Asbury Award for Fostering United Methodist Ministries in Higher Education.

NEW PROGRAMS EXPAND THE REACH OF LEADERSHIP TRAINING

COLUMBIA COLLEGE LEADERSHIP INSTITUTE

In 1989, President Peter Mitchell established the Columbia College Leadership Institute to address the special needs and concerns in developing women's leadership in South Carolina. The college received support from the W.K. Kellogg Foundation that launched statewide meetings in the state's six congressional districts in 1991 and brought some seventy women leaders from around the state to the campus for a weekend retreat on leadership. Special programs highlighted the unique needs of women professionals in a variety of fields. In 1993, the college hosted its first Women's Summit.

President Mitchell envisioned an infusion of leadership initiatives throughout the campus. In 1992, the college approved a leadership studies curriculum. Special leadership scholarships drew new students to the Columbia College campus. The Emerging Leaders Program extended the college's focus on women's leadership to high school girls. Over the years leadership programs have considered the role of women in politics, business, law, ministry, and non-profits.

Among the faculty and staff who have played critical roles in administering Leadership Institute are: Ms. Sara Nalley (first director), Dr. Anne McCulloch, Ms. Kyle

---

35 *Columns*, Fall 1996.

Love, Dr. Diane Thompson, Dr. Mary Frame (first full-time director), Ms. Candy Waites (Director of External Programs), Dr. Trudie Reed, Ms. Roberta Carver, Dr. Sheila Elliott, Dr. Linda Salane, and Dr. Tamara Burk.

WOMEN'S STUDIES PROGRAM[36]

The CC Women's Studies Program was established in 1995, offering "students the opportunity to acquire the knowledge and skill necessary to appreciate and act on these issues confronting the contemporary American woman," according to its mission statement. The idea of the program first began in 1993, when Columbia College was awarded an endowment of $750,000 from the Daniel Estate. The purpose of the endowment was to create a Charles Daniel Chair in History. It was the largest sum of money ever given for an endowed chair at CC. Both the History and Political Science Department and the Human Relations Department decided to present a proposal to President Mitchell and the Board of Trustees in which the money made from the interest on the endowment would be used to establish a Women's Studies program, based in both departments.

A Women's Studies committee was created, with Dr. Anne McCulloch and Dr. Belinda Friedman Gergel representing the History and Political Science Department. Dr. Elaine Kirby Ferrarro and Dr. Linwood Small represent the Human Relations Department. Other members of the committee included Dr. Vivia Fowler from the Department of Religion, Dr. Paula Shirley from the Department of Foreign Languages and Literatures, and Dr. Jerry Savory from the Department of English.

THE HONORS PROGRAM[37]

Chartered in 1984, the Honors Program has provided a rich, academically challenging curriculum and many exciting learning and leadership opportunities for the college's most motivated, talented, and creative students. Distinguishing themselves in countless professional venues and impressive graduate, law, medical, and other post-baccalaureate academic

Dr. Paula Shirley who was instrumental in establishing the Honors Program and served as the first Director shown with junior Rebecca Snyder in the 1986 Columbian.

36 Adapted from an article by Holly Reed, Editor-in Chief, *The Post Script*, September 28, 1995
37 Description provided by John Zubizarreta, professor of English and director of honors & faculty development.

pursuits at prestigious institutions such as Princeton, Duke, Emory, NYU, Columbia, Syracuse, Pennsylvania, Loyola, Drew, Howard, Florida, Oklahoma, Ohio, Tennessee, South Carolina—to name a few recent accolades—our honors students have demonstrated the power of engaged learning, risk taking, reflection, and integrity—all values at the core of honors education at the college. Our students also have helped the program acquire an unmatched national and even international reputation in honors, an accomplishment due in part to the record of our students in making an astonishing number of highly praised presentations at regional and national honors conferences across the United States.

The program's influence extends beyond academics. Honors students have also made their mark as leaders both within and outside the campus, sharing their skills, character, and caring in numerous ways. Involved in campus leadership and activities, and giving generously to their various communities through responsible commitments and service projects, our honors students carry the mission of the program and the college into all their involvements on campus and in the world. From earning collaborative undergraduate research grants to study vital women's issues, to teaching children in Africa with a World-Teach Internship Award from Harvard University, to founding a mentoring program to help local school children improve their educations, to raising funds for disaster relief efforts after natural catastrophes, honors students are routinely at the center of service activities that change lives. After all, embedded in honors is the word honor, which adds responsibility, humane values, and caring to the Honors Program, whose motto is *non magis, sed melior*: not more, but better.

OVERSEAS PROGRAM[38]

Throughout the 1990s, Columbia College provided increasing opportunities for students to study around the world. In July of 1992, Columbia College began offering a new Overseas Program, wherein students would spend a month abroad studying in a foreign university to earn their six semester hours of intermediate language credit. Students studying Spanish and French were eligible to participate in this program. Spanish students studied at the University of Salamanca, with Dr. Paula Shirley as their resident professor. French students studied at the University of Angers, and Dr. Josette Young served as their resident professor.

Dr. Fred Nieto, Chairman of the Department of Modern Languages and Literatures, commented, "They will be able to see and experience firsthand the real language and culture at the same time."

---

38 Adapted from an article by Anne Cooper, staff reporter, *The Post Script*, April 9, 1992.

NEW BUILDINGS ADD TO AN EVOLVING CAMPUS

JOHNNIE CORDELL BREED LEADERSHIP CENTER FOR WOMEN[39]

*Faculty, staff and students celebrate the opening of the
Johnnie Cordell Breed Leadership Center for Women.*

On February 12, 1993, students, faculty, staff and administration gathered on the steps of the new Johnnie Cordell Breed Leadership Center for Women to tour the building and reminisce about the 1964 fire that destroyed Old Main, the building that used to stand in the same spot. Old Main burned to the ground on February 12, 1964; twenty-nine years and $3.2 million later, through the vision of President Peter T. Mitchell and the initial $1 million contribution of Florida entrepreneur Johnnie Cordell Breed for whom the building is named, a new structure was erected that would help the college do what it does best—foster a unique brand of female leadership in the state and maybe even the nation.

The future of Columbia College, according to Candy Waites (who headed the Women's Forum and Leadership at the time), is extremely bright. Waites's work with the Women's Forum enhanced the college's leadership skills by fostering early leadership skills in high school juniors and seniors and through creating a network of women leaders throughout the state. Waites said that her foremost goal for the Women's Forum was to allow "women leaders to get to know one another so that (they) can work together to make positive changes for the state."

One of the most important features of the center will be the Leadership Institute

---

39 This segment was adapted from an article by Trish Willingham in *The Post Script*, February 18, 1993.

which was initially headed by Mary J. Frame.

BARBARA BUSH SCIENCE AND TECHNOLOGY BUILDING

In 1996 a major gift from Janice Suber McNair and Robert C. McNair of Houston, Texas, allowed the construction of a beautiful new science facility. At the McNair's request, the new building was named in honor of former first lady and friend, Barbara Bush, and dedicated in 1997. With its state-of-the-art science and computer labs, student/ faculty research laboratories, and classroom technology, it was and is an exceptional facility.

The new science facilities served as a catalyst for change in the college's science programs. In 1997 faculty began to expand student/faculty research and change instructional methodology. Classroom and laboratory settings became sites of exploration, creative problem solving, and course change. The Science Department received recognition from the

Former First Lady, Barbara Bush, with Robert and Janice Suber McNair, (class of 1959).

National Science Foundation for innovative curricula. Over the next five years, BS degrees in biology and chemistry were introduced, the program underwent successful accreditations from SACS and NCATE, and faculty received two major grants from the National Science Foundation for laboratory equipment and summer faculty institutes and participated, as a faculty unit, in a Maryland DNA workshop.

EDENS LIBRARY

Following the fire of 1964, Dean Thomas Shuler spearheaded a drive for a new library, which was completed and occupied in 1967. Moving day from the old to the new library was set for November 17, 1967. Faculty, staff, and students formed a human chain to pass the heavy books from the door of Vera Young Thomas Memorial Library to the J. Drake Edens Library. Dr. Jesse Shera gave the address at the consecration ceremony on March 7, 1968, and Bishop Paul Hardin, Jr., performed the consecration of the building; the first library then became Alumnae Hall.

STUDENT UNION[40]

Centrally located amidst residence halls and educational buildings, the 35,000 gross-

---

40 Adapted from an article by Erin Armstrong, editor-in-chief, *The Post Script*, August 25, 2003

square-foot Student Union opened its doors to students after a ribbon cutting ceremony on August 26, 2003. The new three-tiered facility features a new state-of-the-art dining hall on the ground level, the Student Activities Department on the lower level, and a student-friendly lounge complete with a coffee shop and outdoor terrace on the top level. "The mission of the building and the purpose of the building is what you'd consider the living room of the campus," said Mark Hall, Vice President for Finance. "One of the things we heard from students—especially those who don't live on campus—is they just want some place where they can sit, relax, and get something to eat between classes."

The Department of Student Activities received an upgrade in terms of space allotted to student organizations through the design of the Student Union. The building itself houses two new conference rooms, which are equipped with tables and chairs and are most comparable to Humphries Hall in size. A smaller conference room is located within the Student Activities suite and can accommodate approximately 20 students around a large boardroom table. The Student Organization Resource Room will also house paper products and supplies available to student leaders, a computer, and furniture for brainstorming meetings and other needs of the organization. Aside from the computer station available to student organizations, the Student Union also features numerous ports for laptop computers.

COLLEGE TRADITIONS[41]

- 1861—Custom of giving each senior a Bible upon graduation began.
- 1909—May Queen Tradition began.
- 1926—First Senior Day: seniors wore caps and gowns one day each week (1930 Senior Day observed with a service in which seniors marched with sophomore sisters).
- 1935—First Miss Columbia College Pageant began.
- 1955—First Ludy Bowl; first senior breakfast
- 1964—First Christmas tree lighting began.
- 1968—First Dad's Night observed.
- 1972—First Mom's Day observed.

---

41 By Holly Reed, reporter, *The Post Script*, March 3, 1994.

CHAPTER 12 — TURN OF THE CENTURY BRINGS A RENEWED OUTLOOK

T he turn of the century brought with it groundbreaking changes and heartbreaking challenges. Nevertheless, the persevering spirit of Columbia College endured, and as always those challenges were overcome.

THE FIRST FEMALE PRESIDENT[42]

In 1997, Columbia College's Board of Trustees selected its first woman president, Phyllis Bonanno, who would become the 15th president of the all-women's school. With a background in international business and politics, President Bonanno's administration emphasized globalization, public service, and diversity.

"It was a very historic moment at Columbia College. It was with a great deal of anticipation that we all looked forward to this moment, and it finally came," history Professor Belinda Gergel said.

Bonanno's lack of higher-education experience didn't seem

President Phyllis Bonanno and students Teresita Alston and Rangeley Bailey in 1997.

---

42 Sources for this segment include: *The State*, May 14, 1997; Associated Press, March 2, 2000; and Associated Press, March 3, 2000.

to bother those who flocked to campus to meet her. Instead, college leaders trumpeted Bonanno's credentials and connections in business and politics. "Phyllis Bonanno believes in the education of young women. She's uniquely qualified to move us to the next level because she's lived it," said Paula Harper Bethea, trustee and chair of the search committee. The college's government board liked her enthusiasm for fundraising and her professional credentials.

Throughout her presidency, Bonanno had a strained relationship with faculty and students. Despite a record number of applicants to the college and an expanding athletics program as achievements under Bonanno's leadership, difficulties within the administration remained, culminating with faculty members putting their concerns about her in writing in February 2000. While no statement was released, top administrators in the college said there were "communication issues." In the same month, campus chaplain Rev. Cathy Jamieson-Ogg asked to be reassigned because she said she did not "fit into this administration." Students had also complained of communication problems.

Dr. James H. Rex served as President of Columbia College during a transition year.

President Bonanno submitted her resignation in March 2000; the same month, Dr. James H. Rex, vice president for development at the college, was appointed acting president by the Board of Trustees.

Rex previously served in administrative posts at the University of South Carolina, Coastal Carolina University and Winthrop College and was a past president of the South Carolina Association of Colleges for Teacher Education.

ANOTHER FEMALE LEADER TAKES THE REINS[43]

On July 1, 2001, Columbia College's new president, Dr. Caroline Bagby Whitson, arrived on campus. The 17th president inherited the leadership of a well-established 147 year-old-college that had weathered trials and experienced many triumphs during its history. But like many small private women's colleges with limited financial resources and endowments, Columbia College confronted daunting challenges and needed reorganization, leadership and focus. With enthusiasm, zeal, ingenuity and a healthy dose of faith in God, President Whitson embraced her new duties at Columbia College and laid careful plans to bring the college into a dynamic new century with a renewed commitment to academic excellence and balanced budgets as well.

A native of Atlanta, Whitson earned BA, MA, and PhD degrees in English from the

---

43   Some material from *The Post Script*, April 2, 2001.

University of Arkansas and a diploma in international relations (awarded with merit) from the London School of Economics. She joined the University of the Ozarks in 1979 and served as director of public information, professor of English and communication, chair of the Division of Humanities and Fine Arts, and vice president for institutional advancement. As provost and vice president for academic affairs, she was responsible for the academic leadership of the 600-student, Presbyterian Church (USA)-affiliated university, with direct supervision of financial aid, athletics, admissions and student life.

President Whitson's new initiatives reaffirmed the United Methodist Church's early intent in establishing the college for service to the church, the state, and the nation and included the incorporation of a day of service as part of Freshman orientation; a monthly campus service program known as CC Serves; and the formation of the Alliance for Women with the South Carolina Commission on Women to address critical issues in women's status in the state. Leadership studies became intricately linked to service in the area of social justice. As President Whitson observed, "Columbia College students know that education should not just be a means to build an affluent life, but should provide the skills and values to build a better world."

President Whitson holds a framed copy of the resolution from the SC General Assembly honoring Columbia College and the Alliance for Women. Introduced by Representative Laurie Slade Funderburk (D-Kershaw County) in March 2006, the resolution was co-sponsored by members of the Women's Caucus and other legislative friends of the college.

SESQUICENTENNIAL CELEBRATION

As Columbia College approached her sesquicentennial year in 2004, President Whitson appointed a special Sesquicentennial Committee that worked diligently to see that the purple and white colors of the college flew for all of 2004 and into 2005. All over the state, church bells were rung for the college, and cakes were cut at celebration events. Astronaut Mae Jemison lectured, author and successful businesswoman Alexandra Stoddard addressed a sold-out audience of over 450 people, Governor Mark Sanford signed a Columbia College commemorative proclamation, and numerous academic departments at the college sponsored special events celebrating the college's

150th year. Former First Lady Barbara Bush returned to the campus to serve as the Commencement speaker.

In its next century of service, Columbia College will build on its past and remains a small independent college for women deeply connected to the traditions of the United Methodist Church. The passionate belief in the potential of educated women to make a difference in society will provide a window to the future. The college's history has equipped it to embrace the challenges of the 21st century with confidence. And the foundation of the school is firmly rooted in the commitment of visionary academic leaders, energetic trustees and community volunteers, dedicated faculty and staff, and thousands of loyal alumnae who have personally experienced the extraordinary world of Columbia College.

DINNDORF THE THIRD FEMALE PRESIDENT

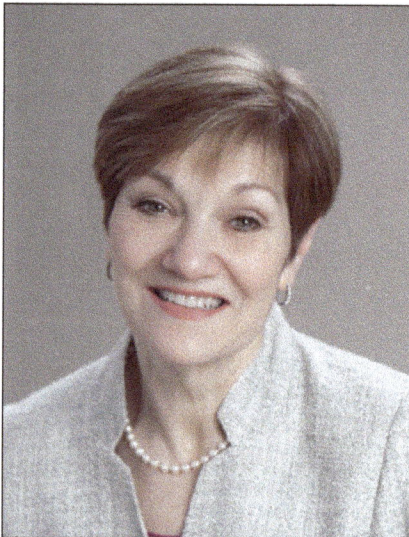

President Beth Dinndorf

On July 1, 2012, Beth Dinndorf, an attorney and business executive with 17 years of leadership experience with a private women's liberal arts college in Minnesota, was named the 18th president of Columbia College.

Dinndorf succeeded Dr. Caroline Whitson, who retired as president on June 30 of that year. Prior to Columbia College, Dinndorf served in a variety of roles on the Board of Trustees of the College of Saint Benedict in St. Joseph, MN, chairing the board from 2010–12 , and serving on board committees dealing with finance, investment, academic affairs, audit, trusteeship and resource development.

She was also formerly a senior vice president and manager of student banking services at U.S. Bank in St. Paul, MN. Before that, she was senior vice president and national sales manager of education financial services at Wells Fargo Bank in Sioux Falls, SD. Columbia attorney Becky Laffitte, trustee and chairwoman of the search committee, described the new president in these terms: "Intelligent, visionary, charismatic, committed, hard-working, spiritual, poised and graceful."

"What intrigued me is that she is not the traditional candidate that one might expect," Laffitte added. "After reviewing her many accomplishments, not only in the banking world but at College of Saint Benedict, I am confident she will elevate Columbia College to the next level."

"She impressed me as a polished executive who has experience in financial matters," said trustee board chairman Lex Knox. "She has an intimate knowledge of and interest in women's education.."

Dinndorf said, "For me, this is the culmination of my career leading businesses, combined with my passion for higher education, and in particular women's liberal arts education."

The school she served so long as a trustee is also her alma mater: she received a Bachelor of Arts degree in mathematics from the College of St. Benedict, and earned her Juris Doctor degree from William Mitchell College of Law in St. Paul in 1982. She is also a graduate of the Pacific Coast Banking School in Seattle.

THE LOYAL SPIRIT OF THE ALUMNAE

Loyalty runs deep in Columbia College alumnae, as former Alumnae Association President Margie Mitchell (class of 1983) well demonstrated: "It's our obligation to ensure that Columbia College continues to provide an outstanding education for young women."

On the day she graduated from Columbia College, Margie Mitchell was comforted by her friend and mentor, Edith Hause. "Why are you crying?" said Hause, then Director of Alumnae Relations, as Mitchell shed tears of joy mixed with a little sorrow. "We're not going to let you get away."

Truer words were never spoken. Since she graduated in 1983, Mitchell's life had been intertwined with her alma mater, and from 2003–2005, she served as the 56th president of the Columbia College Alumnae Association.

"My three years at Columbia College were absolutely fabulous," said Mitchell. "The faculty and staff were outstanding, and I knew I was getting a quality education. I also made friendships that will last a lifetime."

Margie Mitchell (class of 1983), alumnae association president, and Judy Jones Cannon, executive director of alumnae relations, cut cake to celebrate Sesquicentennial Celebration at Washington Street United Methodist Church, the site where Columbia College was originally founded. September 19, 2004.

Mitchell attended Spartanburg Methodist for an associate's degree, and Dr. Ralph Mirse spoke at commencement. "I was so impressed that I decided that I would go to Columbia College to get my bachelor's degree." She enrolled, majoring in business and working part-time in Alumnae Hall, where she became friends with Hause and

Marlena Lewis, Director of Annual Fund. "Edith and Marlena were two of my mentors while I was a student. From them I learned about being committed to the college. They both had a true love of Columbia College."

That describes many alumnae, and it describes Mitchell, as well. Her loyalty to the college runs deep, and during her time as association president she considered herself a goodwill ambassador for the college. "Every alumna has a stake in the future of the college," she said.

PART III:
FOND REMEMBRANCE

A Grand Opportunity

Dr. Michael Broome, Chair of the Department of English at Columbia College, began his career in higher education in the English Department in 1973. He was named dean of the college in 1992 and dean of the Graduate School and Academic Services in 1998.

When I signed my first contract for the 1973–74 academic year, I became part of an English Department that included my close friend and colleague, Bill Mishoe; a teaching legend and Southern literature expert, Sara Mott; an amazingly intelligent Celtic scholar and, at that early time, our Shakespeare teacher, Tommie Workman; our journalism teacher and resident publishing novelist, Barbara Johnson; our calm and knowledgeable professor of German, Mary Hatch; and our new department chair and my personal mentor, Jerry Savory.

The English Department was located then in the Munnerlyn-Beach building, a former dormitory wing attached to Old Main. In 1973, Doc Ariail still tottered over to our building almost daily to retrieve his mail and sit at the desk in his office. What an honor to be able to visit with this veteran of many a classroom and faculty meeting! The Spears Music-Arts Center now occupies the footprint of my first office on campus, and Doc Ariail's ancient desk and overflowing ashtrays are things of the past.

Those days brought recognition to the English department on many fronts, including: curricular revision struggles to ensure that students would have ample opportunities to write and to analyze literary works; the need for a developmental writing facility, which led to our writing lab being established in 1973; Jerry Savory's creation of a program known as the "B.I.G. Major" which defined a new writing emphasis within the English department focused on student preparation for careers in "Business, Industry, and Government."

Dr. Savory's interests and contributions included his publication of *The Vanity Fair Gallery* in 1979; his research on artist Georgia O'Keefe, especially her brief stint at Columbia College; his leadership as vice-president for administration under President Mirse through the 1980s; his acceptance of an interim academic deanship during a time of change in the early 1990s; the incorporation of a writing-across-the-curriculum program into Columbia College's academic structure in the late 1980s; collaborative and cross-disciplinary learning as a vital part of the college's academic identity; and his leadership and determination that resulted in the college receiving a Hesburgh Award for faculty development in 1994. No one meant more to Columbia College's transition to a modern, reputable women's college than Jerry Savory.

One of my fondest early memories involves a day in the mid-1970s when my cohort, Barbara Johnson, came to work with a subtle announcement, which went something like this: "I finished grading two sets of papers this morning, I talked to my husband about a garden idea I have, and, oh, I've learned that Avon Books has decided to publish my first novel." Barbara's first book was a historical romance entitled Lionors and was a follow-up, of sorts, to a seemingly minor character in T.H. White's Arthurian novel, The Once and Future King. This accomplishment gave rise to a number of other historical romances: *Delta Blood, Heirs of Love, Tara's Song, Homeward Winds the River*, and *Echoes from the Hills*.

A significant event for Columbia College around 1980 was the receipt of a Title III grant approaching $1 million, which provided $240,000 for the expansion of our writing lab into a more comprehensive Learning Resources Center (LRC)—consequently enabling us to employ a full-time reading and study skills specialist, Ms. Ann Fleshman, who went on to restructure the LRC into a viable and state-recognized Academic Skills Center, becoming "National Developmental Educator of the Year" in 1996 for her efforts!

Following Bill Mishoe (early 1980s–1990), Charles Israel (1991–97), and Sandra O'Neal (1998–2003), my time as department chair began in 2004, and my goals have centered on building our English education program, promoting the work of the department, and increasing our number of majors overall. When I reflect on the high honor of the chairmanship, I consider the legacy of this College position, stretching back to Dr. Ariail and continuing through my other predecessors. I recall the words of one of my colleagues after he discovered I would become the chair: "Broome, all of those folks in the English Department are smarter than you and they have more class than you have. The best you can do is give them a little guidance, get them the resources they need to do their work, and stay the heck out of their way!"

More recently, John Zubizarreta, Nancy Tuten, Melissa Heidari, Christine Hait, Maria LaMonaca, Stephanie Morris, and Sandra Young joined the faculty, each bringing unique gifts and contributions. These "first teamers" are appropriate inheritors of a strong English Department legacy and are prominent teachers and scholars in their own right.

The man who gave me a job when I really needed one, Dr. R. Wright Spears, stands without peer in his 26-year tenure as president of Columbia College. His strength of commitment in bringing the college back from desperate times, his knack of garnering financial and emotional support for our school, his smile and quick wit, his unbending personal integrity, his spiritual grounding in the Methodist Church—all of these qualities and more define this remarkable leader and educator. Following Dr. Spears was tough, but Dr. Ralph Mirse, in his service as president from 1977–1988, ably improved the college's financial status, increased enrollment, implemented a continuing education component, and positioned academic and administrative programming for expansion of automation facilities. President Peter Mitchell came to Columbia College in 1988 with a vibrant and youthful energy and a clear vision. He was an effective fundraiser, a strong student recruiter, and a firm advocate of women's higher education. President Bonanno, our first female president, supported the growth of our Evening College and graduate offerings, and implemented the Washington Semester, a travel-study program now a College mainstay. As I write this, I am mindful of an announcement by President Dr. Caroline Whitson, of gifts totaling $5.1 million to be used for academic support, athletics facilities, scholarships, and contributions to the endowment. Dr. Whitson's term of office has given us stability, a re-focusing of our stature as a prominent women's college, enhanced leadership programming, and a recognition and celebration of our diversity.

THE SHOW GOES ON:
THEATRE AT COLUMBIA COLLEGE 1959–2007

Sara Nalley graduated from Columbia College summa cum laude in 1963 with a double major in English and speech/drama. After earning an MA in theatre from the University of Florida in 1964 and teaching speech, drama, and English at Dreher High School, she joined the Columbia College faculty in 1976, teaching speech and theatre courses. She served for several years as Chair of the Department of Speech and Drama, and she was a Professor of Communication and Theatre until 2012.

When I entered Columbia College in 1959, I had never considered majoring in theatre. But speech with Mrs. Griffin was my favorite course, and the theatre people seemed to have more fun than anyone else—so, by the end of my freshman year, I was a speech and drama major.

In my freshman year, plays were produced on the auditorium stage in Old Main. My first CC performance was in the revival of Anne Frierson Griffin's *Columbia College Centennial: An Historical Pageant*, first written and produced for the hundred-year celebration of 1954; at the end of every show, I got goosebumps as a solo voice rose singing, "She who has been shall ever be/ Wise good and true eternally."

In 1960, the theatre program moved to the new, beautifully equipped Cottingham Theatre. The theatre opened with another original production by Mrs. Griffin—*Michal*—followed by Gene Eaker's all blue-and-white production of *She Stoops to Conquer*. Then came our first big musical, *Showboat*, with its double-decker boat shining against the new sky cyclorama. More musicals and more plays followed: *Oklahoma!*, *Death Takes a Holiday*, *The Corn is Green*, and others.

At the cast parties that followed every play we sat on the floor at Mrs. Griffin's house, listening to Mrs. G.'s musical voice as she performed *Ol' Miss Brown*: "She wouldn't lay down/ 'Cause if she lay down she would die." We spent weekends earning CC Players points by building flats in the scene shop with Gene Eaker or creating fantasy make-up in the basement dressing rooms with Catherine Eaker. Some of us climbed to the top of the grid above the Cottingham stage to prove ourselves worthy of initiation into Alpha Psi Omega, the honorary theatre fraternity. And at the end of each year we dressed up for the CC Players Banquet, often held on the Cottingham stage.

I graduated in 1963, so I missed the 1964 fire that destroyed much of the campus but spared the theatre. *Arms and the Man* opened on schedule the day after the fire, though some of the costumes had burned and there were no tickets or programs. I'm sure I would have cried along with the cast as Mrs. Griffin told the opening night audience, "I'm glad that we have a comedy to present. Our laughter will be a witness that tonight we are taking a few steps—and that tomorrow Columbia College will walk tall again." The construction following the fire added a 100-seat arena theatre to the second floor of Cottingham, providing a second, more flexible production space, as well as a lab theatre where senior drama majors directed their required one-act plays, with first-year students as actors.

In 1976, I returned to Columbia College as a faculty member in the Department of Speech and Drama. After the death of Mrs. Griffin, who had retired in 1973, the arena theatre was named Griffin Arena Theatre in her honor. Gene Eaker followed her as chair of the department, and Catherine Eaker continued on the faculty as well. Lucille and Rai Baillie joined Columbia College as artists-in-residence. Mrs. Baillie's *Punch and Judy* show, with antique wooden puppets which had belonged to a 19th-century London street magician, became a favorite with audiences. Wayne Bradley joined the department in 1977, and until 2006 he created lighting designs described by our guest artists as equal to those of the best regional theatres.

My first directing assignment, the musical *Dames at Sea*, featured Guthrie Darr's musical direction, Gene Eaker's Hollywood-glitter set, and Lucille Baillie's sparkling silver costumes. In the early years, I directed *Our Town*, *The Effect of Gamma Rays on Man-in-the-Moon Marigolds*, *Story Theatre*, *The Member of the Wedding*, and *Antigone*. Later my specialty became new plays for women: *Talking With* (in which Lisa Wheeler shared the stage with a live snake), *Waiting for the Parade*, *Vanities*, *Eleemosynary*, and others.

During those years the department produced three main stage plays a year. Gene Eaker was our director of musicals: *The Wizard of Oz*, *The Sound of Music*, *Brigadoon*, and *The King and I*, among others. Catherine Eaker was known for her sensitive productions of American plays such as *The Glass Menagerie*, *Ah, Wilderness*, and *Death of a Salesman*. The Eakers founded Gingerbread Theatre, a children's theatre program featuring Saturday morning plays and after-school drama classes that introduced a generation of Columbia-area children to the thrill of live theatre. As I watched a Gingerbread production of *Little Red Riding Hood* one Saturday, the little boy sitting next to me began squirming and tugging at his jacket. Just as the wolf was about to finish off Little Red, he jumped up, threw his jacket in my lap, and yelled, "Hold this, lady. I'm gonna get that wolf!" I'd like to think that that little boy now takes his own children to the theatre.

Many of the students who acted, directed, built scenery, and ran sound or lights at Columbia College are still creating theatre. Donna Drake, who played Dorothy in *The Wizard of Oz*, was in the original cast of *A Chorus Line* on Broadway and continues a professional career as an actor and director in New York. Clarence Felder, one of several men enrolled in the department in the 1960s, acted professionally in New York and Los Angeles before returning to his home state to found the Actors' Theatre of South Carolina. Kay Kaplan Thigpen was co-founder of Columbia's Trustus Theatre, where Jocelyn Sanders is a company member and frequent actor and director. Genie Eaker started The Patchwork Players, a children's theatre company that spent several years in residence at Columbia College. Jenn Colella, who graduated in 1996 as one of our last drama majors, played leading roles on Broadway in the musicals *Urban Cowboy*, *High Fidelity*, and *Chaplin*. Other Columbia College alumnae are involved in professional, community and educational theatre, as well as in television, film, and radio.

In 1995 Catherine and Gene Eaker retired to devote full time to Patchwork Players, and the college discontinued the major in speech and drama. Reconfigured as the department of communication and theatre, it continued to offer a minor in theatre with two productions a year. One of our most popular programs was the Shorts series, an evening of short plays offered each spring. In recent years, our guest director for Shorts was Indira Cureton-Cummings, who as a wide-eyed five-year-old was a regular in Gingerbread Theatre classes and plays. For her, and for all those who have been a part of Columbia College theatre, the show goes on.

COMMUNICATION EDUCATION AT COLUMBIA COLLEGE

Dr. Helen Tate, Associate Professor of Communication, served as the chair of the department of communication and theatre for seven years; beginning in August 2009, she became head of the division of arts and communication studies. She earned a PhD in Speech Communication from Indiana University in 2001.

There's a joke about Columbia College women that goes something like this: you can tell a woman from Columbia College, but you can't tell her much. I have always taken great pride in this insider joke, as I think it says a great deal about the kind of education Columbia College is known for: one that sets our graduates apart from others, but also helps them develop and speak with their own voice. My own journey at Columbia College began in 1999; I knew from the minute I came to campus that this was my ideal job. I felt a part of this small faculty immediately and could not wait to return in the fall.

Sara Nalley was the chair of the department when she hired me, telling me that she thought there might be the possibility to add a major in communication. What she didn't tell me was that she was grooming me to fill her big shoes as chair of the department. The communication program at Columbia College owes a great debt to Nalley's leadership, as she paved the way for the program. When I arrived on campus we had a strong minor program and a central role in the general education requirements as a required course for all students. We proposed a major in communication after urging from the provost and president (and the students), which received approval to accept students beginning in the fall of 2002, though we had several students waiting to declare the major and were able to begin graduating majors the next year. Nalley was a generous and effective mentor who helped me tremendously, and we have one of the strongest majors on campus with over 60 students in both the Women's College and Evening College.

Communication has a long history at Columbia College, going back to its earliest years, and it has been a valued part of the curriculum in many forms over the years; the department of arts and communication studies is just the latest version of this tradition. The 1955 catalogue identifies five academic divisions, including the creative arts; speech and creative writing were housed in that division, along with art, business, home economics, library science, and music. In the years before that, the Department of Spoken English was housed in the fine arts division; in the early-to-mid-20th century, expression, dramatic arts, and physical culture were part of the College of Fine and Applied Arts. While our names and places in the college have changed over the years, the mission of giving women voice through speech education has been constant.

Where are we now? With the generous gift of Roy and Marnie Pearce in honor of his parents, Ann and Tom Pearce, the college established the Pearce Communication Center in 1998, which is dedicated to advancing written and oral communication skills among students and faculty. Director Kyle Love has been with the college in a number of capacities over the years, and her background surely illustrates the value and versatility of a communication degree. Since then, we have welcomed Jason Munsell, Tamara Burk, and Faye Pantsari to the department.

There is constancy in our mission to educate women leaders, now for the 21st century. I am hopeful of a bright future and committed to rebuilding our programs in ways that serve our students' ambitions for many years to come, and while I may not know or even understand the kinds of careers they may have 50 or 100 years from now, I do know that women who develop their voice will be well equipped to lead that change. I think it is safe to say that one will be able to tell a Columbia College graduate for years to come, but not much.

The Road Well Traveled

Elaine Kirby Ferraro graduated from Columbia College in 1970 with a double major in Sociology and Psychology. She earned the MSW degree from Virginia Commonwealth University in 1972 and a PhD from the University of South Carolina in 1991. She joined the Columbia College faculty in 1972 as a half-time Instructor of Sociology and the SC Department of Health and Environmental Control as a clinical social worker; in 1974 she joined the Columbia College faculty full-time.

The one question I am frequently asked is, "How has the college changed since you were a student?" I would rephrase the question, "Has the college changed?"

Yes, the college modernized; voice mail replaced message slips, copiers replaced mimeograph machines. New buildings were built, and old buildings refurbished. Innovative academic programs were added. Each spring a cohort of students leave as alumnae—a bit wiser, more mature, and emboldened by their Columbia College experience. Each fall a new group of students arrives, ready to embark on a journey that will transform them as individuals and unite them as a community. New faculty are hired; some stay, some leave, some retire. Presidents come and go.

Change is constant—but has the college changed? No. The founders established a liberal arts college grounded in the Methodist tradition of service and social justice; that heritage still defines the soul of the college. It was, is, and will be, in the words of President Spears, "a setting for higher yearning." It continues to be a place where women (and men), young and old, find the inner confidence and the outward courage to do what is right in a world where the desire for material possessions and power often overshadows social responsibility; a place where character is measured by words and deeds; and a place where each person is held accountable for creating a community of respect, care, and concern for all the travelers.

The road is well-traveled, the journey marked by new beginnings and endings.

LANNY S. PALMER—THE
COLUMBIA COLLEGE YEARS

Lanny Sullivan Palmer graduated from Columbia College in 1953 in music education, returning in the early 1960s to add a degree in voice performance. She received her MM degree from Indiana University, Bloomington, Indiana, in 1969 and started work on a Doctorate there. She began teaching at Columbia College as an instructor of voice in 1963 and retired as a professor of voice in 2003, continuing to teach part-time until 2007.

When Thomas G. Shuler, my voice teacher at Mitchell Junior College in Statesville, NC, became dean of students at Columbia College in 1951, he encouraged me to continue my education at Columbia College and to pursue a degree in Music Education. I chose to make piano my applied instrument, primarily because of the college's fine piano teacher, Margarette Richards. That was also the year that R. Wright Spears became president of Columbia College. Because he loved music, Dr. Spears liked to be accompanied on his trips by the college vocal octet, the quartet, or a soloist. We students got to know and love President and Mrs. Spears as cherished friends. The trip that I remember most was to New York, when we decided to learn a brand new song, "Carolina in the Morning." The first time we ever sang that song publicly was in Madison Square Garden!

I re-entered Columbia College to obtain a performance degree. Under the guidance of Carolyn Parker I was always challenged to become the best singer I could be. After receiving this second degree in 1963, Mrs. Parker suggested that I remain at Columbia College and assist her by teaching some of her overflow college students that were not music majors as well as teach in the pre-college studio. Here I discovered my niche, for I found I loved teaching voice as much as I loved singing myself.

My first voice student was Margy Oppenlander, a gifted young woman double-majoring in Drama and English. I had often warned her not to leave her music in my studio because it might not be completely safe there. Sure enough, in the 1964 fire her music was totally destroyed, along with my studio and those of Fred and Carolyn Parker, Guthrie Darr, Margarette Richards and Frances Jones, as well as our beautiful auditorium containing our organ and two perfectly matched Steinway Concert Grand pianos. Everyone pulled together in a magnificent way. After the fire, the music department was moved upstairs in the student center as well as into any available room we could find around campus. College Place United Methodist Church helped by providing a place for recitals for the college and pre-college music division. In the fall of 1977 we, and the art department, finally moved into a new facility which was lovingly named the R. Wright Spears Music-Art Center.

In 1965 our department head, Fred Parker, and his wife Carolyn, as well as Frances Jones—one of our two piano teachers—all retired. Guthrie Darr, Miss Richards and I were all that remained of the music faculty. A new department head, Gordon Myers, was chosen; he was a fine baritone, a composer and a specialist in early music, and in addition to heading the department he taught voice and some music theory. Walker Breland, a brilliant organist and pianist was another wonderful addition to our faculty, teaching both organ and advanced music theory. Sidney Palmer directed his first opera for us: *The Medium* by Gian Carlo Menotti. During this time I gave up teaching in the pre-college division and became a full-time instructor of voice at Columbia College.

Dr. Myers left after three years to return to performing, and the same year Margarette Richards retired. James Caldwell, whose doctorate was in music education, was chosen to fill the department head vacancy, and Richard Veale was selected as our second voice teacher. Karen Hudson joined us as the head of the piano department; however, she left the college after two years, and Robyn Gibson took her place. Edmund Shay soon replaced Dr. Breland, teaching organ and music theory, and Neil Andrews joined the faculty as a second piano instructor, later followed by Pawel Checinski, then James Cook and Alan Weinberg.

The new building also inspired an additional direction for the music department: an instrumental music program. A brilliant trumpet soloist, Dr. Randolph Love, was brought in to head this new program. Dr. Caldwell guided the department through the maze of requirements for membership in the prestigious National Association of Schools of Music, while at the same time managing to add a couple of professional degree programs to our department's already growing reputation: in addition to the original BA in music and music education degrees, the college now would offer a professional music degree, the Bachelor of Music.

When Guthrie Darr retired in 1993, after 44 years of teaching at Columbia College, the administration presented him with a well-deserved honorary doctorate. The Columbia College Choir now needed another conductor, and Lillian Quackenbush was engaged as a lecturer in music to direct the choir, the Hi-Cs, and some voice teaching. So strong were her achievements that, when Dr. Caldwell elected to retire in 1999, the music faculty unanimously offered the position to Dr. Quackenbush. Norma Kirkland become head of Music Education, and Edwin Gordon, long acknowledged as America's leading music educator, became a regular consultant to the division and the students.

In 1966, I married Sidney Palmer, whose "day-job" was as executive producer for National and International Productions for South Carolina Educational Television and PBS. The opera program—which he initiated in 1963 as a one-time training vehicle for outstanding vocal students—has been going strong for over four decades. Regularly scheduled costumed opera scenes, which he calls "Opera Can Be Fun!" and one or two staged operas or musical theater productions are scheduled annually.

I officially retired from the Music Department in 2002; Edmund Shay retired in 2003, and Robyn Gibson in 2005. Ed moved to Vermont, while Robyn and I were asked to stay on as adjunct teachers for a few more years. Our beloved friend, Richard Veale, died of cancer in December of 2006. He gave the college, his church, and his friends his full measure of devotion.

Ann Benson, my older daughter, began teaching voice at Columbia College as an adjunct teacher in 2002, and from 2003 to 2006 she was a visiting professor of music; now she is an assistant professor of music. Since 2003, she has been teaching in my old studio. I'm sure she is enjoying it as much as I did!

MY REFLECTIONS AS DIRECTOR OF STUDENT LIFE IN THE 70S

Claire Wilson Yarborough, BA, Columbia College, 1967; majored in religion, minored in elementary education. Director of student life, 1971–77; Board of Trustees, 2006–2010.

The student movement of the early 1960s on campuses across the nation heightened the awareness of student legal rights and responsibilities. Anti-war protests commanding national attention in the early 1970s were as close as the University of South Carolina. No doubt the 1970s ushered in a new era for Columbia College as well. The Judicial Council developed a very sophisticated court procedure; the Dormitory Council made a concerted effort to ensure due process in council hearings. An increasing number of students exercised the right of appeal.

Although change seemed rampant for student life on this quiet campus, the change appeared to reflect the increasing awareness that no man—or woman—is an island. To prevent exposure to the societal issues students were facing would serve only to frustrate the progression that was inevitable as they made crucial life decisions. In a campus environment, students could begin to apply critical thinking skills with the aid of a support system that included residence counselors, faculty, and administrators, as well as their peers. The college's tradition of enriching and encouraging the spiritual growth of students remained central to this analytical process.

Balance was paramount as needed change was sought while honoring the rich history of Columbia College. Consistent with this approach to expose students to critical issues, new programs were implemented. Of special note were the following:

- Women's Awareness, a year-long symposium on women's issues, sponsored by the Office of Student Life and the Speakers' Bureau of CC.
- Peer Advisor League (PAL): an innovative campus-wide program begun in 1976, PAL was implemented to aid in student retention.
- Rape Prevention: a program led by the South Carolina state coordinator for rape prevention, "Rape Crisis" addressed methods of protection and prevention.

Although there is so much more that can be said about the college's history, I will always have my memories of a long parade of "unnamed" women students who exemplified the phrase which appeared on bumper stickers of the era, "COLUMBIA COLLEGE BUILDS THE BEST WOMEN."

Science Department 1972–2002

Dr. Roger Strickland earned his PhD in Chemistry from the University of South Carolina, and was a postdoctoral research fellow at Wayne State University and the Georgia Institute of Technology.

I n the early summer of 1972, I was a research fellow in the chemistry laboratories of the Georgia Institute of Technology when I received a call from my former graduate school mentor at the University of South Carolina, indicating that Columbia College was seeking a new assistant professor of chemistry, and he would like to recommend me for an interview. Several weeks later I visited the campus and interviewed with Dr. Ann Flowers, Dean of Academic Affairs. After meeting with her, President Spears, and members of the Science Department, I knew that I would accept the position if it was offered.

At that time, the science department had four full-time faculty members, including myself, and was housed in the Reeves Science Building. Phil Graef (biology) chaired the department; his biology courses were legendary on campus. His high academic standards and expectations intimidated many students, yet many of those students spoke of the positive effects he and his courses had on their lives years later. Don Mercer, our other biologist, was an inveterate pipe smoker which always alerted you to his location in the building. D.J. Haigler, a physical sciences professor, was a true renaissance man who taught introductory courses in physics, earth sciences, and chemistry. Fortunately, my future teaching assignments were limited to just chemistry.

Paul Rodesiler joined us as an assistant professor of chemistry in 1973, bringing the academic expertise in physical and inorganic chemistry that we needed to complete our chemistry major. Phil and Don had established a solid biology program by 1972, and fine-tuned the curriculum and requirements in that major over the coming decade. Chemistry, however, needed both curriculum expansion as well as laboratory equipment; D.J., Paul, and I focused our attention on developing new courses in physical, analytical, inorganic, and biochemistry. During those years the number of chemistry majors steadily increased as chemistry became a major in its own right.

Don Mercer retired in 1982, and Roger Schmidt joined us as an assistant professor of biology. Roger was a perfect addition to the science program, bringing strong teaching skills in the areas of microbiology and zoology as well as anatomy and physiology, and was also a natural as an advisor. In 1985 the administration and Board of Trustees decided to divide the existing Science Department into two separate departments, biology and physical science. Phil Graef remained chair of biology, and I assumed the position of physical science chair. Sadly, Paul Rodesiler died that same year; Everett Spell joined the physical sciences department as an assistant professor of chemistry. Although his doctoral training was in analytical chemistry, Everett had graduate coursework in physics and astronomy as well. Our program immediately benefited from the variety of courses he could teach. His laboratory instruction was particularly innovative. I especially remember the homemade rockets his physics class used to launch outside our building, with an occasional one finding its way to the surrounding neighborhoods.

D.J. Haigler retired in 1987, and Martha Griffin assumed his position as an assistant professor of physical science, adding strengths in environmental and geological sciences to our program. She immediately implemented earth science courses that were particularly attractive to non-science majors wishing to satisfy science graduation requirements. Her lab experiences were field-oriented, taking students to rivers, swamps, geological digs, and on canoe trips in pursuit of scientific knowledge. After more than 30 years at Columbia College, Phil Graef retired in 1990, and Roger Schmidt assumed the biology chair position while Victoria Hollowell joined the Biology Department as an assistant professor. Her enthusiasm for the subject, tremendous botanical knowledge, and strong encouragement of student research projects strengthened the program considerably. When Vicki left a few years later, Mary Halbrooks joined us for several years, offering expertise in plant physiology.

In the early 1990s, the college administration had begun to develop a master plan for reorganizing academic programs and departments. Numerous changes were made, and one affected the science areas: the biology and physical science departments were re-combined into a single department entitled biological and physical sciences. I was asked to chair the new department and continued in that capacity until my retirement in 2002. As our newly combined science faculty began to plan for the future, Mary Halbrooks left, and Margaret Brinley joined our department in 1994 as an assistant professor of biology. Because the number of science majors had been increasing dramatically—and because a significant number of those majors were expressing an interest in health related careers— Meg had just the academic background we needed. She developed and implemented new courses in molecular biology and biochemistry, established a solid premedical advising program, and guided students in the development of a premedical club. The increasing number of biology majors allowed the addition of another faculty member in 1996, and Sue Carstensen came to us as an assistant professor of biology. Her academic background was rather unique: not many think of kudzu as an object of scholarly study; however, it had attracted Sue's interest as a graduate student and became the focal point of her research. After joining our department she enthralled us with kudzu stories and even treated us to home cooked kudzu in a variety of forms!

After that, our faculty remained constant until my retirement, though we often employed adjunct instructors to assist with introductory courses. One very significant event in our departmental history had yet to occur: the Reeves Science Building, built in 1962 and containing classroom space and science laboratories, clearly needed updating. In 1996, a major gift from Janice McNair (class of 1959) and Robert C. McNair of Houston, Texas, allowed the construction of a beautiful new science facility. At the McNairs' request, the new building was named in honor of former first lady and friend, Barbara Bush, and dedicated in 1997. With its state-of-the-art science and computer labs, student/faculty research laboratories, and classroom technology, it is an exceptional facility, and served as a catalyst for change in our science programs. In 1997 we began to expand student/faculty research and change instructional methodology. Classroom and laboratory settings became sites of exploration, creative problem solving, and course change, and we were honored to receive recognition from the National Science Foundation for our innovative curriculum. Over the next five years we introduced BS degrees in biology and chemistry, underwent successful accreditations from SACS and NCATE, received two major grants from the National Science Foundation for laboratory equipment and summer faculty institutes, and participated, as a faculty unit, in a Maryland DNA workshop.

A Brief Historic Perspective of
Physical Education (1950 to Present)

Dr. Richard Krejci is an associate professor and chair of the Physical Education and Health Promotion department. He came to Columbia College in 1983. He has an undergraduate degree in teaching physical education, a master's degree in health education, and a PhD in public health.

Anyone familiar with the physical education department at Columbia College knows of the dedication and longevity that was awarded to Lucile Godbold, affectionately known as "Miss Ludy." Lucile served the college for an amazing 58 years (1922–80). She was referred to as the "physical education department" and did not have any significant assistance in teaching activity classes until around 1950. Miss Ludy was unconditionally dedicated to Columbia College right up until the time of her death back in 1981.

According to the 1950 Bulletin, the day enrollment at the college was 181 students. At that time, Lucile Godbold was an associate professor and chair of the physical education department; she also coordinated the athletics program. Students were required to complete over eight credits of physical education courses consisting of all forms of marching, games, and exercises to promote good posture and to maintain physical fitness. PE courses that were offered in 1950 included field hockey, basketball, volleyball, softball, archery, and tennis. Students were also able to satisfy their physical education requirement by participating in competitive team sports.

In 1954, Miss Ludy established intramural flag football games between different dormitories. The teams with the best records ended a season with a playoff in the "Ludy Bowl."The games were first played on the field between the Ariail-Peele Administration Building and the west wing dormitory known as Munnerlyn-Beach; in 1964, the Ludy Bowl was played on the smoothly raked ashes of Old Main, and it made the front page of The State newspaper. The Ludy Bowl soon moved to the Eau Claire High School athletic field, and later games were played at Hammond Academy before being permanently brought to the campus in 1987, after the campus athletic field was completed. Today the Ludy Bowl is played on the Younts Soccer Field.

By 1960, Miss Ludy had been promoted to a full professor. While enrollment was growing, the physical education requirements and department goals had remained the same over the past decade. There was, however, the addition of several new physical education classes including modern dance, folk dance, body mechanics, and others.

In 1970, the PE requirement had been reduced to four consecutive semesters of one credit activity courses. Additional courses were offered in ballet, karate, horseback riding, and kickball. The Porter Gymnasium was completed in 1971 through a generous gift in memory of Mrs. Julia Inabinet Porter by Mr. and Mrs. Cary C. Boshamer of Gastonia. The adjoining Greer Natatorium, built in honor of Jacque Greer (class of 1971), was also completed through a gift given by her parents, Mr. and Mrs. W. Jack Greer of Greenville. That year, the physical education complex was dedicated to Miss Ludy and officially named the Godbold Center.

In 1970, Mrs. Sylvia Seymour Davis (class of 1966), an instructor of dance, was hired to assist in teaching the activity courses; she established the college's first dance company over the coming years. In 1972, Phil Hodges was hired and became acting chair of the department, whose name had changed to the department of physical education and recreation. Phil spearheaded the addition of new recreation courses, including scuba diving, equitation, snow skiing, and ice skating, as well as new aquatics courses in lifesaving and synchronized swimming. Deborah Parramore was hired in 1972 and established the Poseidon Club, which remained competitive until the late '80s.

Just two years after his arrival on campus, Phil Hodges was in a terrible automobile accident, and his injuries prevented him from returning. He was replaced in 1974 by Bruce Curtis, who brought to the college the major and certification to teach physical education and health in elementary and secondary schools. There were four emphases in the PE major: general physical education, aquatics, dance, and recreation. New theory courses were added to the curriculum as well. In 1975, a new dance-arts major was also established.

Dr. Curtis remained the chair of the department until the arrival of Joann Kemp in 1978, who hired several new faculty to support the relatively new PE major; these included Linda Rikard, a curriculum specialist who coached tennis and established the summer swim program for children in 1980. In 1982, the department was reorganized again, becoming the department of physical education and dance. I arrived at Columbia College in the fall of 1983, and in my second year was asked to start a campus wellness program with programs and activities for the faculty and staff.

The department was split in 1985 into separate departments for physical education and for dance. In 1992, I was appointed to the position of chair of the PE department; that same year it changed its name to the department of physical education and health promotion (PEHP). The emphasis in the general education requirement had begun to shift from team and individual sports to personal fitness with an emphasis on lifetime physical fitness and health. In the college's strategic plan of 1993, President Mitchell asked the PEHP department to eliminate the physical education major and to focus on a single general education course in wellness and fitness. We created a course entitled "Wellness and Lifetime Fitness," which remains the primary course offered for students to meet the general education requirement in health and wellness.

In 1999, with the departure of the athletics coordinator, Kim Shibinski, athletics became an individual administrative department, moved from under the PEHP department and reorganized under the direction of the vice-president for enrollment management. Today Columbia College is an active member of the National Association of Intercollegiate Athletics (NAIA) Region 14. Athletic teams include basketball, soccer, tennis, and volleyball; Ana Oliver (class of 1998) has been the director of athletics over the recent years. Karen Donald Tanner served as the first athletic director.

Today the PEHP department offers a minor in health and wellness, designed to prepare students to work in companies that offer personal health/fitness activities and/or wellness programs for their employees and to help prepare students to study in advanced degree programs in related fields such as health administration, wellness programming, exercise science, physical/occupational therapy, recreation therapy, and administration of nutrition education programs. The general education requirement is two to three semester hours in one of two course options: wellness and lifetime fitness and/or the women's health seminar.

Back to Business

Mary Hutto and Mona El Shazly

The rudiments of the Department of Business and Economics have existed for most of the history of Columbia College. The department offered students a two-year degree in secretarial science until 1976, when Margeurite Toyne was hired to redesign the business curriculum to reflect the trend of encouraging women to enter business and accounting careers. Dr. Toyne developed a four-year business program emphasizing management and requiring students to complete an internship placement. (This requirement placed Columbia College at the forefront of business programs in the state and continues to date to set our graduates apart from other institutions.) At that time, the department staff consisted of Dr. Toyne and Cecil Bierley, a long-time professor of secretarial science and business writing courses.

In 1979, Jim Bouknight replaced Dr. Toyne as department head, leading the department for four years and expanding course offerings, including the addition of the accounting major. Department faculty grew to include three new members: Becky Oatsvall Shaffer for accounting, Mary Hutto for marketing and management, and Lark Adams to instruct economics. In 1985, Jim Bouknight left for further academic study, and the college offered Mary Hutto the position of department chairmanship. In the next few years, our enrollment in business administration and accounting soared, with over 300 majors at one point. Recruiting and maintaining the appropriate faculty was demanding; during these years, we added Dave Day in management, Jane Clarke in accounting, Mona El Shazly in economics, and Louisa Harrell in accounting.

The growth of the Department of Business and Economics represented a tremendous shift in the dynamics of the college. As a liberal arts-based institution, having two-thirds of the student body majoring in a professionally oriented field (business administration, accounting, and education) presented the college with challenges and opportunities. Compounding this shift was the growth of the Evening College which offered majors in business administration, accounting and public affairs. The department's physical location moved from a small free-standing house (our "little hut") to the third floor of the Allison building, then to our current location in the Breed Leadership building.

In 1992, Dave Day accepted to serve as interim department chair for one year, until Howard Sanders joined us in 1993 and took on the department leadership until 1999. In an effort to be innovative, we began a major and minor in entrepreneurship and hired Susan Davis in 2001 for that program and to direct the Center for Women Entrepreneurs. Due to low enrollment, the entrepreneurship major and minor were dropped—but we continued to offer a number of courses as business electives for both accounting and business majors.

In 2000, Mona El Shazly stepped in as department chair, with core faculty remaining intact until Dave Day retired in 2003 and Louisa Harrell in 2005. In 2004, Laurie Mozley was hired as departmental coordinator, and in 2006 Yuan Li was appointed as management professor. Harry Cooper, who taught business law and ethics as an adjunct professor, took on additional responsibilities in 2005 by serving as evening college advisor. The department now also houses the Columbia College Center for Economic Education, which provides teachers of grades K–12 with resources to improve classroom instruction in economics and finance.

MATHEMATICS, MANAGEMENT, MARKETING, MONEY, & MORE

J. Joseph (Joe) Mitchell—BA, mathematics, Wofford College; MEd, mathematics, University of North Carolina; DEd, (Honorary) Sungshin University. Retired from Columbia College in June 1999.

In September 1961, I entered a wooden-floored classroom in Old Main as an optimistic, excited, and nervous young professor. On my second day of classes, I received a comforting pat on the back accompanied by these words: "Welcome, Mitch. Everything is going to be all right, my boy!" That assurance from none other than Doc Ariail lifted my spirit and confidence, further confirming my acceptance into a caring academic community. A similar statement by President R. Wright Spears has also not been forgotten: "When you get to the place when you have no nervousness before teaching a class, you may have become too overconfident."

For the next 11 years, most young women found mathematics difficult or not enjoyable, and seeing even a few students in each class exceed their expectations or change their attitudes became my goal and provided ample reward. Of course, being able to compare lesson plans and pedagogy with my departmental peers, including Annye Elizabeth (Betty) Welch and Estella Long, added to my professional growth and confidence.

Just before the unforgettable fire of 1964, our mathematics department had moved into the Reeves Science Building. The mix of science and mathematics disciplines set up an interesting and fun academic "tug-of-war" regarding which was the purest science: biology, chemistry, or mathematics. Since my office was adjacent to Phil Graef's biology lecture room, I always waited each term until hearing him deliver his "purest science" lecture—spotlighting biology, of course. In turn, I followed with my counterpoint mathematics lecture the next day in my classroom which was adjacent to his office. This friendly struggle continued for years and often prompted side debates during our coffee breaks involving professors Graef, Don Mercer, D.J. Haigler, Jack Bedenbaugh, and me.

Quite suddenly, my career took an unexpected turn when, in May 1972, Anne Flowers, dean of the college, asked me to assume the position of registrar, with allowances to continue teaching mathematics classes occasionally. The Registrar's office had two experienced staffers, Frances Smith Owens (class of 1964) and Louise Abney Hinnant Watson (class of 1939), each of whom exercised patience and understanding as I transitioned into my new role. Further support was provided by William Butler, then serving as assistant dean, and Ray Sharpe, director of admissions. We became quite a busy team as we initiated and instituted numerous procedural and policy changes affecting our related areas of responsibility. I recall a three-week period that first summer, when the three of us worked very late hours and weekends to write, layout, design, and publish the *Columbia College Bulletin*, which had to be available to students and faculty before classes began in September. None of us knew that it was an impossible task, so we did it!

Upon my return from vacation in late July 1976, the automobile of William Butler, then the dean of the college, was parked in front of my home. After a few greetings, Bill informed me that he and President Spears wanted me to assume the position of director of admissions and records (the combination of registrar and admission director). Again, I was very thankful that Frances Owens (class of 1964) was fully prepared to become assistant registrar, virtually taking over the day-to-day operation of that office—for most of my time had to be devoted to the development of a viable admissions and recruitment marketing program. The admissions office had several capable staffers including admissions counselors Nancy Eldridge Rawl (class of 1967) and Skeet Wylie Clarkson (class of 1975).

Without good students in sufficient numbers, the college would soon be in financial crisis. Fortunately, several new positions were filled as funds permitted, thus helping effect an upturn in new student enrollment. While I cannot recall everyone, I remember the outstanding contributions of admission counselors Marian Kinon Hanna (class of 1977), Janet Rauch Keen (class of 1980), and Julie Breland, as well as transfer counselor Sylvia Gray (who also was general office manager).

Another career surprise came in late spring 1983, when President Ralph T. Mirse informed me that my friend and colleague Bob Barham, long time business manager/VP for business affairs and treasurer, would be moving to a position in the office of development. I was honored to be offered the VP/treasurer position and accepted it with enthusiasm. The dean of admissions position I had just vacated was filled by David Maltby who became a good friend and colleague.

The new position I assumed was vast, challenging, and rewarding. The 56 people on the business affairs team can, of course, be credited for most of successes attained; at the risk of omitting some outstanding team members for their exceptional hard work, skills, and dedication, several persons I recall and commend are Buddy Courtenay, Dan Johnson, Cliff and Marie Hill, Richard Brown, Sara Mason, David Singletary, Ruth Dixon, Thelma Dugosh, Lula Edwards, Tony Pickett, and Stan Watson. Further, I was very fortunate to be able to work closely with several Board of Trustees members whom I highly respected and who, along with Dr. Mirse and later, Peter Mitchell, challenged and supported me. They include Leon Goodall, Gary Daniels, Sara Brabham Eastman (class of 1942), Bill Sellars, Ted Walter, Ed McDowell, Jack Hupp, and George Fant.

About two years after Peter Mitchell became president, he began restructuring the administration. In July, 1990, he asked me to assume the position of vice-president/ dean of enrollment management. This was a position with which I was familiar, having previously directed admission and recruitment operations. Still etched in my memory is President Mitchell's penetrating challenge: "Always remember the importance of your new student enrollment goals, for the first year you fail to reach them, one of your staff will be fired. The second year in a row YOU will be fired, and the third year I will be fired!" Fortunately we always met our goals, thanks to our very strong, goal-orientated staff—which included Charlotte Stackhouse Broome (class of 1975), director of freshmen admissions; Sylvia Gray, director of transfer admissions; Doris Harrell (class of 1990), director of financial aid; Julie Arseneau King (class of 1988), admissions counselor and assistant director of freshmen recruitment; admissions counselors Else Villalba Cole (class of 1992) and Leigh Owen (class of 1987); Nita White, admissions operations assistant; and Alice Hood, financial aid assistant.

After a 38-year career with Columbia College, I retired on June 30, 1999. Each of the positions I had held was challenging, interesting and fun. At my retirement reception, I felt it quite fitting to close with the following quote from Tony Bennett: "If you enjoy your work, you won't work a day in your life." During my entire career at Columbia College, I can count on my 10 fingers the days when I did not look forward to going to work.

From Bob Barham

Bob Barham served as business manager and treasurer of the college, and later as associate vice president for development.

After a very difficult period in the late 1940s, the college began to show a dynamic improvement in the early 1950s under the splendid leadership of the Rev. R. Wright Spears, who was appointed president in 1951, and Dean Thomas G. Shuler who came to the college at the same time. Enrollment began to grow rapidly, finances improved, new faculty members were added, several new buildings were erected—indeed, the whole atmosphere of the college had changed. The college's administration was reorganized to handle her growth and to perpetuate her acceptance throughout South Carolina Methodism and in high schools and junior colleges. It became necessary to develop plans to secure funds to enhance programs, add new offerings to the curriculum, and continue the overall improvement of the school.

During the early '50s, the president secured the services of John E. Hills to be business manager and treasurer. Mr. Hills did a superb job in all his areas of responsibility and was ably assisted by Clarence Dixon, accountant and assistant treasurer; Judy Banks, his secretary; and Madeline Allen, cashier. Mr. Hills left the college in the fall of 1960; at that time, President Spears appointed me to be the new business manager and treasurer of the college, a position I was to hold for 23 years. I was fortunate to have Mr. Hills' staff to work with me for my first 10 years in office.

From 1960–63, we made progress in most areas of the college's business and financial life. Then on Wednesday, February 12, 1964 at about 2:00 a.m., a horrendous fire destroyed Old Main, the adjoining East Dormitory, and a large part of West Dormitory. This brief period witnessed magnificent cooperation and hard work on the part of all in the Columbia College family, the people of Columbia, and beyond as we prepared for the students' return. Classes resumed on Monday, February 17.

Mr. Dixon retired in 1970 and was succeeded by Dan Judd. Miss Banks also left in 1970 to be married. In 1975 Mr. Judd resigned to form his own accounting firm, and we were pleased to promote Mrs. Allen to office manager and accountant. Assisting her were Lula Edwards (1968–88) and Thelma Dugosh (1975–95). Joe Mitchell, who had served the college superbly as professor of mathematics and later as registrar and dean of admissions, was named to succeed me as vice president for business affairs and treasurer in 1983, and I was named associate vice president for development.

Mrs. Allen retired in 1985 and Dave Singletary assumed the position of office manager. At about the same time, Stan Watson was named assistant to the vice president for business. In 1990, Mr. Mitchell was named vice president for enrollment management and later as dean of admissions. He was followed as vice president for business affairs and treasurer by Linda Salane. Robert Waites was named to follow Dr. Salane in 1994, with the title of vice president for administration; Mr. Jeff Maddox became executive manager of business affairs.

In 2002, Mark Hall was appointed vice president for finance, and Jenny Ricker became director of administrative services. Tom Hoffmeyer assumed duties as the college accountant. John Jones succeeded Mr. Hall as vice president for finance in 2004. At that same time, Beth Westbury became the college comptroller.

Although not officially a part of the business office staff, special thanks and commendations are due two ladies who were the "voices of Columbia College" for many years as they worked the switchboard with great skill and politeness: Elizabeth Dowling and Lois Klemy will always be remembered with much fondness and appreciation.

FOUR DECADES OF HISTORY AND POLITICAL SCIENCE AT COLUMBIA COLLEGE

Bob Moore

The year 1960 was one of meager new beginnings for the department of history and political science. In that year Dr. Spears, Dean Shuler, and department head Harry Harvin hired me, fresh from the doctoral program at Boston University, and part-time instructor Selden K. Smith, still in the doctoral pursuit at the University of South Carolina. Before I arrived for the fall semester of 1960, Dean Shuler asked me to be acting head of the department because Dr. Harvin had resigned. Selden and I were to become the slender threads of continuity in the department for the remainder of the millennium. (Selden once quipped that together the two of us have one pretty good memory—so I consulted the other half of my memory for this essay). From that meager start, by the year 2000 the department was composed of a half-dozen excellent professors led most capably by one of our own graduates, Belinda Friedman Gergel (class of 1972). Selden and I had retired, and the one constant in history—change—was evident.

The 1960s were tumultuous and exciting times: the civil rights movement was sweeping the country, ultimately to affect a Columbia College that was unenthusiastic about the change. A survey in October 1962 revealed that only 10% of students and 60% of faculty favored desegregation of public schools; 6% of students and 63% of faculty thought integration of the college would be good. That year, the annual conference of the South Carolina Methodist Church resolved that Columbia and Wofford Colleges must remain segregated by race; however, the conference in 1963 reversed that resolution and resolved to place no restrictions on their colleges' admission policies. That opening was welcomed by President Spears, who was working with city officials and community leaders to gradually make the transition away from a segregated society. By 1966, the college made a tiny but profound move by admitting one black student: Lillian Irene "Bunny" Woods was the perfect person to break that 112-year history of "whites only." Though she left the college after a year, later graduating from the University fo South Carolina, she opened the way for more black students at Columbia College in succeeding years.

The concept of academic freedom was rather underdeveloped in South Carolina in the 1960s. Several professors at the university and other colleges had been dismissed in the '50s because their racial views didn't square with the patterns of segregation in the

South. Selden and I were active in the South Carolina Council on Human Relations, an organization dedicated to racial justice and thus to the dismantling of the oppressive system of segregation. Dr. Spears supported our activities, and our efforts to engage students in the Student Council on Human Relations and in the conferences sponsored by the Christian Action Council, which had similar aims.

Not all academic freedom issues concerned race. The Vietnam War was an emotional issue that tore at friendships and institutional loyalties and resulted in pressure to conform to the pro-war agenda of the government; many equated opposition to the war to sympathy with communism. I think all of the professors in the department during the '60s were opposed to the war to a degree. The most dramatic flare-up concerned an anti-war coffeehouse on Main Street opposite the city hall. The city sued to shut it down as a public nuisance, and two Columbia College professors were subpoenaed to testify: both Selden Smith and English professor Raymond Moore gave testimony supporting the coffeehouse and its right to dissent on the war issue. The board was alarmed and summoned the two professors before a committee to determine whether they were fit to teach at Columbia College. Smith had received his doctorate from USC. and had been awarded tenure. Raymond Moore didn't have tenure and was dismissed.

During the 1960s the college grew, and the department usually had three full-time faculty and an occasional part-time person or visiting professor. In the early '60s, Florence Sherriff taught in the twilight of her career. Replacing her was James W. Campbell, near the beginning of his career. After three or four years, Carlanna Hendricks replaced Campbell and was soon joined by Ruth J. Cunningham. These two dynamic and extremely articulate women immediately became very popular teachers, motivating many of our students to aspire to become accomplished women like them.

In the late '60s, the department initiated practicum and internship experiences for our students, awarding students academic credit for participation in practical work experience. We placed students in government offices, civil rights organizations, chambers of commerce, archives and manuscript libraries, political campaigns, law offices and other venues. The department sought to serve the community as well. For example, we helped organize tutorial programs for disadvantaged pupils in poorer sections of the city. One year, some 50 C-Square students were involved in tutoring at the Bethlehem Community Center and Carver Elementary School. We also organized bringing underprivileged children, black and white, to the campus for art lessons taught by students and supervised by Dr. Dawson Zaug, head of the art department.

We entered the 1970s without Carlanna Hendricks, who moved with her physicist husband to Francis Marion University for the remainder of their careers. George Pruden served as visiting professor for two years, beginning in 1970. Ruth Cunningham moved away in 1974, and Sam Holliday came on that year, staying until 1976. We realized that the Department must broaden its scope to serve the new needs and desires of the students. We identified a number of courses as a pre-law curriculum, and also organized a public affairs major—an interdisciplinary set of courses designed to prepare students for employment in government, law, charitable organizations and community service. To strengthen our political science offerings, we hired Shirley Geiger in 1978, our first African-American faculty member. The following year Gloria Durlach joined the department. After two decades heading the department, in 1983 I resigned, and Dr. Mirse appointed Selden, who became a superb department head.

Richard Gergel was one of many distinguished adjunct professors our students enjoyed over the decades. One of Richard's students in the Introduction to Law course was Helen Nelson (now Grant, class of 1981), who later returned to Columbia and enjoyed a distinguished career in the law as a partner with Gergel; she later served as chair of the Board of Trustees for the college. Judges serving as adjuncts include Hon. Joseph F. Anderson, Jr., US Circuit Court, Hon. C. Tolbert Goolsby, Jr., SC Court of Appeals, and Hon. Alex Sanders, also of the SC Court of Appeals. USC professors who have shared their talents with us include Donald Fowler, Daniel Hollis, Richard Chowan, Bill Foran, and John Benfield. The director of the Columbia Urban League, J.T. McLawhorn, has taught a course on the current state of African-Americans in South Carolina for several years.

The 1990s were years of rich development for the department. Anne McCulloch joined our faculty in 1989, replacing Gloria Durlach, and helped us initiate a new political science major. Another professor was necessary to support that program, and we were fortunate to be able to hire Dr. Sheila Elliott. In the meantime, Dr. Belinda Friedman Gergel (class of 1972) had come into the department, first as a part-time instructor, then adjunct, and finally as a regular faculty member. Selden and I felt great pride in having one of our own as a colleague. These three women were instrumental in the development of the college's Leadership Institute and the new Women's Studies Program created in cooperation with the department of human relations. The Department gained an endowed chair in history when the family of Charles Ezra Daniel contributed $750,000 for establishment of the chair in his honor; I was first to hold the honor, then Anne McCulloch, and now Tandy McConnell.

The look of the Department's faculty at the beginning of the new millennium gave evidence of progress: Belinda had become chair; Tandy McConnell was our new specialist in European history, and became chair of the department after Belinda retired in 2001. Hyman Rubin III took my place teaching American history in 1999. Ed Sharkey joined the faculty when Anne McCulloch began administering the Evening College. Mary Ann Mahony taught Latin American history in 2002–03, and when Sheila left Sharon Jones came to teach political science.

What augurs well for the Department's role in the college and in the community and state is the strength of its faculty. This faculty is composed of excellent teachers who are also publishing scholars. If the professors can maintain their excellence in teaching while also publishing and contributing to their community, then the department and the college will continue to grow in strength and reputation.

EDUCATION DEPARTMENT HISTORY

Dr. Rebecca Glover Swanson (class of 1957); Dr. Mary Steppling, Chair, Education department

When asked to write this "history" of the education department, my first thoughts were of the years 1953–57 when I was a student at the college and no actual "department of education" existed. One could minor in education, and all were counseled to get a teaching credential "to fall back on." All of us from that time remember Mary Lois Staton and Miss Gilly (Julia Guillard); we took child growth and philosophy of education, followed by only six weeks of observation and teaching.

In the late fifties, departments were placed into divisions; teacher education was division V. Dr. Staton was Chair and Walter Fries had joined the faculty. Cleo Parks, who later became dean of students, was also listed as an assistant professor in the department. It was during this time that the college was SACS accredited for women, as well as being a member of the Association of American Colleges and the National Association of Schools and Colleges of Methodist Churches. The first Education Club was established during this time, also. The 1957–59 college catalogue contained photos and a listing for the education department.

In the early '60s, William Crowley had been added as an associate professor. There was a division then between elementary education and secondary education, and speech "correction" was located in the department of speech. Frank Elliot was chair of the department, and other faculty included Crowley, Walter Fries, Virginia Ann Flowers, and Evelyn Fullbright. The Education Department was re-divided into elementary education and a department of special studies, with Flowers and Fullbright, respectively, as chairs. Special education, speech correction and library science were now in the special studies department. Owens Corder was prominent in developing the special education major while John Devens worked hard to establish a strong major in speech correction. Helen Jordan helped spearhead the effort in library science.

Part of my job was to coordinate the early childhood education program, which included supervision of the "new" off-campus kindergarten. Sarah Dawsey contributed greatly to the growth and development of this program, taught for years in the kindergarten itself, and taught occasional classes in early childhood education. By the fall of 1969, Ann Flowers was dean and Gene Piner was brought in as chair of the education department, with Miriam Rawl, Rebecca Swanson, Joe Browde, Bob

Moore, and Sarah Dawsey as professors in the department. Dr. Piner advanced the department significantly, while Imogene Lipscomb became chair of the special studies department.

Excellent leadership was given under the capable direction of Ronald Midkiff, who brought numerous ideas and an innovative vision to a newly emerging department. Education became the Center for Developmental Studies; new course choices and new certification options were made available to students. Faculty included Dr. Elliott, Dr. Lipscomb, Dr. Browde, Dr. Hallman, Dr. Isaac, Dr. Rawl, Dr. Swanson, Dr. Baud, Miss Burns, Miss Dawsey, and Miss Jordan. Don Patenaude was added, as well as Edna Earle Christmas. The special studies department became a part of a unified department of education. During Dr. Midkiff's tenure, the department became accredited not only by the state of South Carolina, but by the National Council for the Accreditation of Teacher Education (NCATE); this accreditation brought acclaim and prestige to the department and to the college. During this time, the education department also became a member of the prestigious American Association of Colleges of Teacher Education.

In the late '70s, the Center for Developmental Studies was changed back to the education department. Dr. Rawl succeeded Dr. Midkiff as department chair, and Linda Herlong (Collier) joined the faculty, along with Jennifer Lewis (Mungo) and Debbie Brady. Dr. Rawl and Dr. Swanson worked tirelessly to start a graduate program in education.

In 1980–81, Dr. Rawl became dean of students and vice-president of academic affairs. Dr. Swanson became interim chair and ultimately chair of the department of education, with a tenure that covered over 15 years. Dr. Rawl continued her sustained support for a graduate program; under her leadership, master's degrees were established in education, music, and English. At the same time, the Library Science major in the undergraduate program was discontinued. Over the coming years, the education department provided support and leadership for certification programs in departments including art, dance, physical education, music, biology, chemistry, English, social studies, French, and Spanish.

In the late 1980s and early '90s, the department's active, high profile involvement in a national teacher education reform effort was maintained. During Dr. Mirse's tenure, the education department was awarded a competitive grant to establish a Center of Excellence on Campus, with Jennifer Mungo as director. The speech correction program, led by Beth Ingram, Bonita Dowell, Leigh Ann Spell, and Mary Steppling became known by the more accurate term, Speech-Language Pathology. An adopt-a-school partnership was made with nearby Arden Elementary School in 1988–89, under the coordination of Helen Wise.

Through President Mitchell's leadership, Columbia College was the recipient of a major grant from the Bell South Foundation. Through the ensuing program, core curriculum revisions were made to focus on "the teacher as leader." Sharon Ray joined the education faculty to direct the project and assist with course work. Another grant spearheaded by President Mitchell, funded by the Knight Foundation, affected the entire Columbia College community, with the education department playing a major role in the project—which allowed the department to add Anna McEwan, Mary Frame, Darrel Garber, and Liz Jones to the faculty.

Directed teaching has become the culminating field experience, rather than six weeks of observation and teaching as it was in 1957. Students are sought after by school administrators, recognized for the excellence and leadership their training has secured for them. When the college, during President Whitson's tenure, asked that each degree program incorporate leadership concepts, the education programs were already aligned with this initiative. The Education department continues to thrive! It remains the largest department on campus, with hundreds of graduates who have served well in cities and communities across our state and nation.

The Department of Religion & Philosophy

Vivia Lawton Fowler graduated from Columbia College in 1976 with majors in religion and sociology; she received an MA in Religion from the Lutheran Theological Southern Seminary in 1980, and a PhD in Philosophical and Psychological Foundations of Education from the University of South Carolina in 1994. She was a member of the Department of Religion and Philosophy from 1986–2007. She was named president of Wesleyan College in 2017.

I n the final chapter of Dr. Jerold Savory's *Columbia College: The Ariail Era* (1979), President Ralph T. Mirse suggests that "the reputation of the college as a church-related institution—at least among its own teachers, students and constituents—will hinge directly upon the academic reputation of its teaching of religion" (237). If the reputation of Columbia College in the second half of the 20th Century hinged on the reputation of its department of religion, the college must give credit to three men whose combined tenure in the department covered well over 120 years: George P. (Pat) Chandler, Harris H. Parker, Jr., and Charles G. (Chuck) Pfeiffer. Relative newcomers lead the department now, but the legacy of Chandler, Parker, and Pfeiffer continues.

During a 1952 stopover in Columbia to visit an old friend, Harris Parker received an invitation from Dr. Spears, then the newly-selected president of Columbia College, to join the faculty. Dr. Parker's contributions to the department are legendary; he developed the college's Center for Contractual Studies and was author of numerous mission statements, official documents, and annual prayers for the opening of the academic year. His course, Death in Religious and Cultural Perspective, was always the first of the department's courses to fill, and after his retirement in 2000 he continued to teach that course each semester for another seven years. In 1959, Parker was joined by Chuck Pfeiffer, who led the department as its chairperson from 1959 to 1986, when he was succeeded by Parker. Pfeiffer challenged students to read the Bible carefully and analytically, fascinated students with the study of Native American religions, and was well-known for his devotion to students. Pat Chandler joined the faculty in 1967, and students were drawn to his caring but frank demeanor, often coming to him for advice and conversation about controversial and complicated issues during the sometimes-volatile '60s. Pat offered significant contributions in scholarship and leadership to several professional organizations, including the Conference on Christianity and Literature and the South Carolina Association of Religion. Religion students from the 1950s will also remember Margaret Dukes, who taught in the department from the late '40s until 1953, and Andrew Eickoff who joined the department for a few years in the mid-'50s.

In 1986 I began to teach a couple of courses for the department and in 1989 I joined the department full-time, succeeding Parker in 1994 as chairperson of the department. In 1998 I relinquished the chair to Pat Chandler, who retired in 1999. Rowan Crews joined the department in the fall of 1999, taking the chair—and with the official retirement of Harris Parker in 2000, Lisa (Sister Catherine) Unterseher joined the faculty. Crews and Unterseher led the department's next curriculum reform. In 2007 Crews turned over the leadership of the department to Unterseher.

During the '60s, students took two semester hours each in Old Testament, New Testament, and Introduction to Religion. In the 1970s, they were required to complete three semester hours each in Biblical Survey and Introduction to Religion. After a curriculum revision in the '80s, students were allowed to choose one biblical and one nonbiblical course from a menu of courses—and with the general education revision of 1999, the religion requirement became one course chosen from a menu of courses that include biblical and nonbiblical courses.

In the mid-1960s, William Butler joined the department and contributed philosophy courses to the department's offerings. Later faculty, including Pat Chandler and another chairperson of the human relations department, Linwood Small, also taught courses in philosophy. After the death of Dr. Butler and the retirement of Dr. Small, the faculty approved moving the philosophy minor to the religion department. Adjuncts taught philosophy courses until 2005, when the college approved a position for a philosopher: Omar Bozeman served as visiting professor of philosophy from 2005–07, and Heather Matthusen assumed the position in 2008.

As proud as we are of our dedicated, scholarly faculty, we are even more proud of the wonderful students who have majored and minored in religion, philosophy, and Christian education over the years. Many have furthered their studies in graduate schools and seminaries around the country, frequently obtaining prestigious scholarships for their post-graduate studies. Many serve churches as clergy and lay leaders; others are employed in social service and community service agencies.

The Department of Religion and Philosophy has a bright future as it continues to develop courses and programs to create, using the words of President Ralph T. Mirse, "a more religiously literate society" (Savory 237). Always willing to experiment with active learning techniques, from team teaching to role-play to technology to biblical character presentations, the department seeks to make the study of religion and philosophy both relevant and rigorous. The department will continue to accomplish this goal in the future through dedicated faculty, willing adjuncts, caring support staff, and inquisitive students.

A Work in Progress

Stephen Nevitt, Chair, Department of Art

The earliest mention of art courses found in old college bulletins was in 1864; the description for the drawing and painting department included the following statement:

> Pupils pursuing these arts are taught the principles and practice of design. It is the aim of the instructor to render the study interesting, and, at the same time, to correct and refine the taste, and to excite an artistic spirit.
>
> DRAWING. This embraces lead pencil, monochromatic, crayon, and colored crayon.
>
> PAINTING. Embraced in this are fruits, flowers, landscape, and figure in pastel and oil.
>
> Proficiency in these arts will alone entitle to a diploma in this department.

The 1883–84 college bulletin description for the school of art includes the following:

> The object of this school is not merely to impart knowledge but to awaken and cultivate a love and appreciation of the fine arts. The course will embrace linear and perspective drawing, painting in water colors and oil, and ornamental work.
>
> A commendable enthusiasm and a generous rivalry has been awakened among pupils of this school. Several drawings and oil paintings which were on exhibition at commencement attracted marked attention. Testimonials of excellence were awarded to Miss Ella Brown, Miss T. Elwell and Miss Mary Stack.

The earliest evidence found for the current BA major in art was in the 1951–52 college bulletin. The list of courses offered by the department includes studio, art history, and art education. This bulletin includes the following statement:

> The art department of Columbia College is an integral part of the liberal arts system, and, as such, is not intended to take the place of a professional art school. Its aim is to give the student a well-rounded training, including an understanding of the various branches of art, of draftsmanship, of pictorial

presentation and its limitations, of non-objectivism, surrealism, etc., and their limitations, and above all, to encourage creative thinking and productivity. It is the belief of the department that such a broad background of basic knowledge of both traditional and contemporary techniques will greatly increase the possibility of full expression and, later, will leave the student free to approach his problems from a philosophical point of view.

The most famous former faculty member in the department of art was Georgia O'Keeffe, who taught briefly during 1915. According to lore, O'Keeffe was not particularly happy here, but her time at Columbia College was important; she was not pleased with her work when she arrived at Columbia College, believing that it reflected too much influence by the teachers with whom she had studied. She packed up previous works, vowing not to look at them again, and began to work on a series of charcoal drawings that were different from things she had done before. After completing a number of these, O'Keeffe sent them to a friend in Charleston, requesting that her friend look at the works and give an opinion, and asking that her friend not show the drawings to anyone else. The friend liked the drawings and sent them to Alfred Stieglitz, one of most prominent gallery owners in New York City and an important photographer in the history of American art. O'Keeffe and Stieglitz eventually married. If we look at the drawings done by O'Keeffe at Columbia College, we perhaps can see early suggestions of her mature style. She befriended Dr. James Ariail during her time here, and they kept in touch after O'Keeffe's departure.

I began teaching at Columbia College in 1976. The chair of the department was William Tidwell, a kind and gentle man whose encouragement and advice were much appreciated. Also on faculty was Vicki Pullen (class of 1969), who eventually became chair of the department. A number of other faculty members have come and gone through the years, including William Campton and Diane Buck. Dr. Campton reinvigorated our art education program and developed highly effective courses of study in three-dimensional areas. Dr. Buck prepared a number of wonderful art teachers who are making significant contributions in the public schools of our state. Dr. Buck also was a gifted artist in ceramics and continued the development of courses in three-dimensional studio areas.

Current full-time faculty members include Mary Gilkerson, who joined our faculty in 1991 and has taught a wide variety of courses with primary emphases in painting, graphic design, photography and first year two-dimensional design and color theory; and Ute Wachsmann-Linnan, who joined the faculty in 2000 as a full-time art historian. Another important member of our art staff in recent years has been Jackie Keane Adams, a graduate of the college, who came on staff here in 2005 to help with the gallery.

The Spears Music/Art Center opened in November of 1977. By the mid-1970s, we had in place a very modest BA degree program in studio art (27 semester hours of requirements in art) with an option for teacher certification. During these years, there was a strong interest among our majors (and their parents) for marketable skills in art. In addition to art education, the department began to reflect a growing emphasis on graphic design and the development of internships in a variety of areas.

A strong interest for accreditation by NASAD emerged during the early 1990s, and the pieces seemed to be in place to apply for membership. During the 1991–92 academic year, we completely revised and upgraded the curriculum for the BA in studio art with NASAD standards in mind. We were awarded associate membership in NASAD in April of 1996, only the second school in the state to be accredited by NASAD. We were notified during the spring of 2003 that we had been awarded full membership.

Through the years, two families have been wonderful supporters of the college and great friends of the department of art: the Lipscombs and the Goodalls. Guy Lipscomb and his family are well known for their support of the arts in South Carolina. The Goodall family has been very important to our program also. Together these families have provided the financial and moral support to advance our art department, and its respective programs, considerably over the years.

The most important part of my Columbia College experience by far has been our students. I can think of few things in life which bring me greater joy than to see a former student drop by my office or to receive an e-mail, a note, or a phone call from one of them. During recent years I also have had the privilege of seeing daughters of a few former Columbia College art majors enroll to study art here, which is flattering and also a bit humbling.

History of Columbia College Student Health Services

This article was compiled by Mary Ann Young, director; Thelma Graham, staff nurse/ coordinator of medical records; and Brenda Greene, administrative assistant

In 1952, travel was not as convenient as it is now; most students did not have cars, and some students were from poor families in South Carolina, so transportation home became a problem when a student became sick. Wil Lou Gray (class of 1903) was instrumental in establishing the infirmary (which was later named for her) so that students would have a place on campus to be cared for when they became ill. Jane Bruce Guignard, a prominent physician in the city, was the campus physician for a period of time, having an office in downtown Columbia and coming to campus several times a week to care for students. Virlee Fanning, RN, served as director from 1954 to 1980. Students could be examined 24 hours a day by the nurse, and if they had fever or other symptoms of illness would remain in the infirmary in order to be seen by the physician.

After Dr. Guignard's departure, Dr. John Holler served by contract with the college to see sick students during the week until he retired in 1982, after which Serina Clark served as the campus physician. Directors of health services after Mrs. Fanning's retirement included: Margaret Latham, RN, Cindy Gilbert, RN and Pat Boyleston-Coleman, RN. Dr. Larry Hedgepath was the college physician for a short period, and donated medical equipment as well. Dr. Stacey Brennan became the college physician and medical director from 1982 until 2003. Dr. John Nash succeeded her until he retired in September 2004, at which point Dr. Christopher Hutchinson accepted the position.

With the conversion of Fleming Residence Hall to an administration building (now Allison Administration), the infirmary was moved to the rear portion of the first floor. Mary Dial, LPN, worked evenings and Grace Corley, RN, worked the overnight shift. The infirmary discontinued the overnight services in 1990, changing the hours from 8:00 a.m. to 8:00 p.m. Monday through Thursday, and 9:00 a.m. to 4:00 p.m. on Friday. Carol Rothstein, RN assumed that position and continued to work until Spring 1995. The number of student visits averaged around 1800 a year, due to the policy that students could receive class excuses for illness—a practice that was discontinued in the 1996–97 academic year.

In January 1995 Mary Ann Young, RN, CSN was named director of health services. After months of assessing the needs of the health center, Young sought ways to make the center more efficient and provide more comprehensive health care for students. During the 1996–1997 academic year a clinical laboratory improvement amendments (CLIA) permit allowing provider-preferred microscopy procedures to be performed was obtained, making laboratory services easier and more convenient for students. In 2000, documentation of immunizations (MMR, TD and PPD), along with medical insurance verification were required as part of the registration process; students who did not have record of their immunizations could receive them in the Health Center. Young's leadership led to reorganization of the infirmary, beginning with a name change to Student Health Services. Evening hours were eliminated and clinics were held three times per week. Student Health Services evolved as a place where student's health needs were met, educational information was shared relating to a student's specific problem, and students had a comfortable environment enabling them to reveal health problems for treatment.

Young's vision, with the assistance of staff nurse Thelma Graham, was to serve the students in the most practical, cost-effective, high-quality delivery of care that could be achieved with limited resources. Young took the initiative to pursue accreditation of health service, becoming the first nurse-directed small college student health center to receive accreditation by the Accreditation Association for Ambulatory Health Care in 2001. After the second accreditation term in 2004–07, Student Health Services had evolved to become a comprehensive women's health center, providing increased health education and services for students until its closure in 2010.

Department Of Modern Languages & Literatures

Dr. Paula Shirley

When Columbia College's first students registered for classes in the fall of 1860, the curriculum was a classical one, reflecting the academic mores of the time. In addition to subjects such as grammar and literature, young women took Latin and had the opportunity to study Greek. The study of modern languages was available, but limited: German and French were offered, with French being dominant. As the 20th century advanced, the modern spoken languages began to overshadow classical ones, and eventually students could choose among French, German, and Spanish. The approach to language study was radically different, however, from current approaches: for almost a century, grammar and translation were emphasized over the spoken word. That changed in the late fifties, as communicative methods more grounded in the culture of the language being studied began to prevail.

Enter Aracelis G. Shaw. A native of Cuba, Dr. Shaw had immigrated to the United States; in 1958, she joined the faculty of Columbia College. Now the most-studied language in the United States, Spanish had been considered much less important than French. Dr. Shaw helped to change that perception; in addition to her active teaching of the language, at the college she founded the Spanish House for resident students who wanted to "live" the language.

When I arrived at Columbia College as a young assistant professor in 1978, Dr. Shaw had already been here 20 years, Paul Ponsard almost ten, and Dr. Walker only a few. The number of majors in Spanish and French was quite low, but we forged ahead, trying to recruit interest. I put on a one-act play in Cottingham, *Las Aceitunas*, starring Spanish majors, with the Eakers and Lucille Baillie from the theater department collaborating on costumes and a set. I proposed teaching a course in Mexican-American literature, a rather new field at that time, especially in the Southeast; as part of this, Josefina Niggli visited the campus, presenting a master class in acting to theater students.

The 1980s saw a burgeoning interest in travel/study. Paul Ponsard and I were eager to organize tours to our countries of interest, France and Spain, and took advantage of Maymester to lead numerous groups of students abroad. From Paris to the Riviera, from Madrid to the southern tip of Spain, Columbia College students savored two great European cultures and languages. When Josette Young joined the faculty in

1980, she added variations to the offerings by taking groups skiing in the French Alps during the winter break and to Québec, as well as leading May tours through France.

During her many years, Dr. Shaw brought strong leadership and innovations to the department. In 1987 another dynamic leader joined the faculty and took over the helm of the department on Dr. Shaw's retirement: Fred Nieto. A native of Uruguay, Fred brought new energy and direction to the department, especially regarding our "study abroad" programs. Fred established close relationships between the college and the University of Salamanca and The University of Angers, France. The first group of students to study in Salamanca left in summer of 1992. I happily accompanied them on their journey, meeting Fred in Salamanca; his knowledge of the city and university paved the way for marvelous experiences for all of us.

During the 1990s, many cultural and research projects occupied our attention, such as the semester we hosted Senegalese writer-in-residence Aminata Sofal, an exchange realized by Josette Young. In addition to Sofal, we invited other artists to share their talents with our campus community, including Ron Hudson, guitarist, and Francesc de Paula Soler, a Spanish guitarist and musical innovator. And never let it be said that foreign language professors eat boring food! Musical events, awards programs, and many other departmental gatherings feature foods of France, the Francophonie, and Latin American countries. Fred Nieto's Brazilian feijoada has brought tears of joy – and tears of sorrow when he retired and we said farewell to his cooking. I even prepared Cuban black beans, rice, and ropa vieja (literally "old clothes") for an honors class on Cuba.

Our department has involved itself in many rewarding activities. In 2000 Josette Young received a grant from the Eisenhower Professional Development Program—Foreign Languages to offer two programs, one in Foreign Language in the Elementary Schools and another to teach technology for the foreign language classroom. Beth Droppleman received a State Department of Foreign Languages grant in 2004 to teach FLES methods to teachers. In 2004 I had the honor of teaching for a semester at the American University in Bulgaria as the recipient of a Fulbright Scholar Award. The most recent outstanding scholarly achievement highlights Beth Droppleman, who published a reader with Molière & Company; a classroom text entitled *Les Lais de Marie de France* in 2007.

The department of modern languages and literatures has always been an international department, in the sense that our faculty has a strong global perspective and experience—but we also have drawn in members with multinational heritage, including: Joanna Machaj de Vargas, a native of Poland married to a Mexican; Corinne Mann-Morlet, a French-American with a lifetime of contact with France; and Rocío Zalba, a native of Argentina, who works on contemporary Latin American theater.

The department is lively with a full complement of dedicated professors. What marvelous opportunities the future will hold as the city and state change. Columbia College is a special community with the warmth, steadiness and commitment to transform women's education. It still has much to teach its women and our department looks forward to a continuing, strong role in that effort.

Dancing My Path at Columbia College Straight from the Heart (of Charleston Motel)

Martha Brim is a professor of dance at Columbia College and artistic director of The Power Company, the professional dance company in residence at Columbia College.

I joined the dance faculty at Columbia College in the fall of 1983 having never before been to South Carolina. After visiting friends and family in Orlando, I traveled to Tallahassee and was invited out by Nancy Smith-Fichter, my former mentor in the FSU Dance Department. Nancy said, "Libby Patenaude called me today from Columbia, SC and is looking for someone who can teach modern dance technique, dance composition, history, pedagogy, etc." Someone in our party said, "How about Martha?" I decided that I should check it out. I researched the Columbia College Bulletin and was intrigued. I set up the interview and made plans for a detour to South Carolina to check out Columbia College.

As a part of my interview for the job I taught an audition class, after which I remember sitting on the floor in the Godbold Dance Studio with two students, Merrie Goldson and Tracey Mathias. I had lots of questions myself about Columbia College, including "what is it like to attend an all-women's college?" I believe it was Tracey who replied to my question, "There are plenty of guys down the road at USC. Plus you don't have to get dressed up for class." That simple answer satisfied my curiosity and I moved on to my next question—but as I have reflected on that moment since, I realize how much more there is to that identity, and I am a bit astonished to recognize how much it has influenced me as an artist, teacher, and citizen of the world. It turns out the dance department at Columbia College was an ideal environment for me to enter as a young artist. That studio, the setting of my first impressions of dance at Columbia College, is more than the birthplace of numerous choreographic masterpieces and creative catastrophes, alike; it has been the core from which an extraordinary collection of women (and men) have practiced the distinctive blend of creativity, collaboration and community, that rare alchemy of spirit, for which dance at Columbia College is so well known.

I was offered the job. Libby Patenaude hired me, the chair of what became the Columbia College dance department. Looking back, I can't imagine a better mentor. I learned so much from Libby about ambition while being a good and fair person. Libby's drive, passion for life, integrity, shrewd intelligence, and vision are inspirational.

Before I came on the scene, there were influences along with Libby whose names bear mentioning: Mary Martin, Sylvia Davis, Donald Blumenfeld-Jones are a few I recall. Libby's tenure of leadership in the dance department marked significant achievements in the arts, not only for Columbia College, but statewide as well.

In 1996 a serendipitous event took place: Nancy Smith-Fichter (who recommended me for the job at CC) was retiring as chair from FSU, and Libby was offered the position. At first this felt more devastating than serendipitous—but her replacement, Susan Haigler-Robles, brought a fresh perspective and new dynamic energy to the department until around ten years later when she moved on. Susan is a force of wild unconventionalism and inspired us all toward new and courageous directions. Both Libby and Susan earned their undergraduate degrees from Columbia College, studying dance and going on to pursue graduate and doctoral degrees only to return to Columbia to lead the dance department that fueled their passion for dance as students.

Carrying that unique vision forward has been Wrenn Cook, who has skillfully chaired and advocated for the dance department in a time that has become increasingly difficult. We are now called to envision a renewed curriculum and exist in a new structure as Columbia College moves toward organized divisions and away from the old departmental structure. There are many people who have offered their hearts and souls to the work of the dance department; those who have served as full-time dance faculty and have not yet been mentioned are Patty Graham, Brenda McCutchen, Linda Caldwell, Christian Von Howard, Allison Tipton, Chase Angier, Ginny Skinner Haynes, Donald Shabkie, Michael James, Jill Zupan, Robin Prichard, and Marcy Yonkey-Clayton.

I owe a debt of gratitude to Columbia College for allowing me the opportunity to dance my path as I have developed a career as an artist and academician while creating and cultivating many treasured friendships and collegial relationships. And it's not done yet.

PART IV: APPENDICES

APPENDIX A: A BRIEF HISTORY OF THE ALUMNAE ASSOCIATION

Organized on June 21, 1882, the Columbia College Alumnae Association is the fifth oldest in the United States. A small group of graduates met in the college parlor to establish The Columbia Female Alumnae Association with the goal of raising funds to purchase walnut furniture for the parlors. Since that time, alumnae have supported the college through gifts of time, talents, resources and commitment.

Prior to 1922, all alumnae financial support was applied to the college General Fund. Then for a period of time, alumnae gifts were applied to the college Endowment Fund. In the 1950s the Quint Club was instituted and alumnae were asked to contribute five dollars a year. In 1957 the Loyalty Fund replaced the Quint Club placing more emphasis on the loyalty of alumnae to support the college through both unrestricted gifts and later through gifts to the endowment. In 2000, The Loyalty Fund was again designated to only reflect unrestricted gifts from alumnae that are applied to the General Fund.

Following the devastating fire of 1964, the college Board of Trustees challenged the Alumnae Association to raise $100,000 for the Rebuilding Campaign. Alawee Gibson Tucker (class of 1939), then President of the Alumnae Association, with the help of the Director of Alumnae Affairs, MaryAnn Smith Eubanks Crews (class of 1959), accepted the challenge. On Alumnae Day, June 5, 1965, Alumnae Association President Alawee Tucker announced gifts and pledges from alumnae far exceeding the original goal and eventually reaching a total of $422,000.

To express appreciation and to honor alumnae, the Board of Trustees agreed to change the name of the Vera Young Thomas Memorial Library to Alumnae Hall when the library was moved into a new campus building. A portrait of Miss Thomas and recognition of the original name of the building hangs in the Parlor of Alumnae Hall. MaryAnn Smith Eubanks Crews (class of 1959), Director of Alumnae Affairs, worked with Janet Alexander Cotter (class of 1956) and Nancy Williams Johnson (class of 1955) who were appointed by Alumnae Council to co-chair the committee that planned and implemented the renovation and decoration of the library reading room into the Alumnae Hall Parlor. It is decorated in a formal manner reminiscent of the Stackhouse Parlor of Old Main. Alumnae Hall Parlor has provided a lovely setting for many college and alumnae events.

Until 1958 the employment of an Alumnae Secretary was irregular because of financial shortage. Miss Emma Wright was the first person employed by the college to work with alumnae from 1926 to 1928. Mrs. Barney Owens (Sarah Bolt) became Executive Secretary from 1937–39. She was followed by Mrs. B.R. Nichols (Merrell Bennet) from 1940–41 and Miss Christine Smith, 1941–42. The college could not continue to fund this position so until the mid-1950s the work of the Alumnae Association was carried out by many dedicated alumnae volunteers. During the mid-1950s under the presidency of Dr. R. Wright Spears, a full time director of Alumnae Affairs was hired and the office was funded by the college budget as it continues to be today.

Marjorie Faucett Patterson (class of 1949) served as the director of Public Relations and Alumnae Affairs from 1949–51 succeeding Mrs. J.M. Ariail (Belva Haynsworth) who had served for a year as a part time alumnae secretary. In 1952, Mrs. Ruth Lightsey served as the head librarian and also handled Alumnae Affairs until Janet Alexander Cotter (class of 1956) was hired as the alumnae secretary in 1957 serving through 1958. Nancy Williams Johnson (class of 1955) followed her serving as alumnae secretary until 1963. She was succeeded by MaryAnn Smith Eubanks Crews (class of 1959) who served as the director of Alumnae Affairs until 1970. Carol Ann Lee (class of 1966) filled the position until 1971 and was followed by Gale Rigby Phillips (class of 1969) who served until 1974. In 1974, Edith Collins Hause (class of 1956) was hired by Dr. R. Wright Spears to become the director of Alumnae Relations. These were followed by: Charlotte Stackhouse Broome (class of 1975); Edith Collins Hause (second term of service); Marlena Redfern Lewis (class of 1964); Judy Jones Cannon (class of 1974); Lisa Kennerly Livingston (class of 1991); Sara Snell (class of 1999); and Carla Lewis Moore (class of 1994).

Since 1926, alumnae representatives have served on the Columbia College Board of Trustees, self-study committees, presidential search committees, Medallion committees, the Alumnae Council, and fundraising committees including all major capital campaign committees. Also, the Alumnae Association president participates in every college commencement service to welcome the newest members upon their graduation. Many alumnae have served as commencement speaker.

The Alumnae Association has presented to the college many of the portraits which are displayed on the campus. These portraits have recognized outstanding service to the college by alumnae, faculty, staff and friends.

One of the most treasured traditions is Alumnae Day and Alumnae Weekend. Some of the activities include the annual business meeting of the Alumnae Association, presentation of the Distinguished Service Award, the Wil Lou Gray Outstanding Educator Award, the Career Achievement Award and the Outstanding Young Alumna Award. The presentation of the senior class doll, recognition of the outstanding faculty member and election and installation of the Executive Committee of the Alumnae Association also take place during the annual meeting. Another highlight of the morning is a coffee that honors retired members of the faculty and staff. During the Saturday luncheon, the reunion class with the highest percentage of attendance is recognized before each class gathers for a class photograph and meeting. Each year the class celebrating their 50th reunion is honored with a lovely luncheon in Alumnae Hall Parlor on the Friday of Alumnae Weekend. The Decorating Committee of the Alumnae Council provides beautiful decorations for the occasion and the Special Events Committee prepares and serves the food, all of which is indeed a labor of love.

Alumnae Weekend programs have changed over the years to meet the changing needs of all alumnae, but this special event still provides an opportunity for the renewal of friendships and continued involvement in the life of the college.

The annual Faculty and Staff Christmas Coffee hosted by the Alumnae Association is an expression of love and appreciation to the college family. The Alumnae Hall parlor is beautifully decorated by the Decorating Committee and the delicious food is prepared and served by members of the Special Events Committee.

Additional plans, events and traditions of the Alumnae Association and the Alumnae Office are reported in chronological order from 1977 through 2016:

1977

- September: Alumnae Association dedicated the back entrance hall of Alumnae Hall as the Mary Blue Spears Parlor, in honor of the wife of Dr. R. Wright Spears.
- The alumnae merchandising program began.

1978

- May 12: A groundbreaking ceremony was held to build a gazebo that would be called "The Columns." This fulfilled the promise that was made by Alawee Gibson Tucker (class of 1939) and MaryAnn Smith Eubanks Crews (class of 1959), to rebuild the columns after the fire of 1964. The board approved the concept. Mrs. Tucker made a gift to pay for it and Mr. Zach Daniels, plant engineer at the time, built it.
- The first national telethon was conducted on the campus in Alumnae Hall by the Alumnae office. This telethon was held annually until 2005 when it was replaced by a year round call center located in the Breed Leadership Center and

named in memory of Janie Farmer Myers (class of 1937).

- The Student Alumnae Ambassadors was organized to provide a liaison between the students and alumnae. This has proven to be a very successful program connecting the alumnae association to the campus.
- The first Alumnae Recruitment Committee was established. All areas of the state were represented by alumnae volunteers who assisted with identification and recruitment of good prospective students. Alumnae throughout the southeast hosted receptions and dinner parties to provide opportunities to meet and discuss Columbia College.
- A grant was received to computerize all alumnae and development records. Up until this time all mailings were done by an old addressograph that produced labels that were applied manually and prepared in zip code order for the post office.
- Dr. Ralph T. Mirse and his wife, Blanche, became the president and first lady following the retirement of Dr. R. Wright Spears and his wife, Mary Blue Spears. The alumnae office secured alumnae volunteers to host dinners and receptions throughout the southeast to introduce our president and his wife to all CC constituents.
- The Alumnae Association decorated and maintained a college guest house for many years near Maxwell House, which has served as the president's home.
- The Alumnae office for many years assisted the Music department in planning choir tours throughout the southeast. Alumnae volunteers arranged performances, housing, and meals for the Columbia College Choir.
- The Alumnae Association established a new tradition to recognize outstanding alumnae contributions through the "Distinguished Service Award" at Alumnae Weekend. This award is presented to an alumna selected on the basis of character, service to family, church, community, and college.

1979–80

- The college approved the position of assistant to the alumnae director in 1979 and Cindi Floyd White (class of 1977) was hired.
- The Alumnae office promoted the sale of the book: *Columbia College: the Ariail Era* edited by Dr. Jerold J. Savory of the English Department.
- The Alumnae Association was involved in many ways during the celebration of the 125th birthday of the college. Some of the activities included a luncheon and program for all former student body presidents. All alumnae clubs undertook the project of refurbishing the student lounges in dormitories.
- The Alumnae office has always been involved in the production of the alumnae

magazine which has had several different names but is now called *Columns*. Class news, marriages, deaths, memorials, and some alumnae articles are among contributions provided to the Public Relations Office.

1980–81

- At the fall meeting of the Alumnae Council, a portrait of Vera Young Thomas was dedicated and hangs in Alumnae Hall. The portrait was given by members of the Thomas family.
- The Loyalty Fund Committee began writing personal thank you notes for gifts to the college, a project that has been most effective.
- In 1981 *Heart to Heart*, a book of devotions written by alumnae, was compiled and printed by the Alumnae Association to be given to all students.

1981–82

- In 1982, the Alumnae Association celebrated 100 years of service to the college. Many activities were planned throughout the year: on January 31 there was a reenactment of the founding of Columbia College at Washington Street United Methodist Church in downtown Columbia. SC Governor Richard W. Riley issued a proclamation in honor of the Columbia College Alumnae Association. The 50th Class Endowed Scholarship Fund was established for classes celebrating their 50th reunion and presented to the college during Alumnae Weekend; the Centennial Committee presented a skit to the student body depicting the founding of the Alumnae Association. In 1982, a centennial quilt was designed, produced, and presented to the college and hung in Daniel Dining Hall. A holly tree was planted on the campus by the Association; and on April 10 the pageant, "The Spirit of Columbia College" was presented in Cottingham Theatre followed by a reception in Alumnae Hall.
- The annual tradition of honoring an outstanding faculty member by the Alumnae Association was begun with Dr. Sara Mott as the first recipient.
- Alumnae were actively involved in the college's New Horizons Campaign which had a goal of $5 million for the endowment.

1983–84

- The 1983 *Columbian* was dedicated to the Alumnae Association.
- The class of 1933 was the first class to make a gift of $11,000 for their class endowed scholarship.

- In 1984 the Alumnae Association established the Career Achievement Award to recognize an alumna who had distinguished herself in her career.
- In 1984, Edith Hause was promoted to vice president for Development and Charlotte Stackhouse Gamble Broome (class of 1975), assistant to the director, was promoted to the director of Alumnae Relations.
- MaryAnn Smith Eubanks Crews (class of 1959), president of the Alumnae Association from 1983–85, presented the idea of a "Surcie Shop" and a committee was appointed on the Alumnae Hall Committee to work on it. Proceeds were designated to maintain the Alumnae Hall Parlor. Betty Ulmer McGregor (class of 1951) served as the first chair. Margaret (Meg) Ward Pace (class of 1962), who served on the original committee, eventually became the chair and continued to serve for over 30 years. The shop is currently located in Daniel Hall foyer and has proven to be a great success, thanks to dedicated alumnae volunteers.

1986–90

- In 1986, the first *Alumnae Directory* was published and sold to alumnae.
- Dr. Ralph T. Mirse retired in 1988 and Dr. Peter T. Mitchell became the 14th president of Columbia College.
- The New Horizons Campaign is successfully completed exceeding the goal by $1.5 million, increasing our endowment threefold.
- In 1989 after the successful endowment campaign, Edith Hause requested to return to full-time alumnae service work and was appointed vice-president for Alumnae Relations by President Mitchell with the approval of the Board of Trustees.
- Alumnae annual support had increased 100% over the last 14 years.

1991

- The Alumnae Office and the Career Planning and Placement office began a new program utilizing alumnae volunteers to provide career networking services for students. The volunteers will speak with students about specific career choices and preparation for the job market.
- Lisa Kennerly Livingston (class of 1991) is hired as the assistant director for alumnae and development. Lisa had been a student worker in the Alumnae office during her four years as a student.
- The Fine Arts Committee of Alumnae Council was restructured and became the Alumnae Recruitment Committee. These volunteers would assist the Admissions Office in recruiting new students. Although the format has changed

through the years alumnae continue to successfully assist in the recruitment of students for the college.

1992–93

- The Alumnae Association honors Cliff and Marie Hill for over 27 years of service to the college as head of the food service program. A portrait of the two of them was presented to the college, to hang in Daniel Dining Hall.
- Major renovations to Alumnae Hall were completed adding additional office space and a new columned façade fronting on Colonial Drive. Alumnae Hall is the oldest building on campus, originally built in 1922 as the library.
- The Johnnie Cordell Breed Leadership Center for Women was dedicated in April 1993. Alumnae Council, the governing body of the alumnae association, had outgrown the available meeting space in Alumnae Hall and began holding meetings in Breed Leadership Center.
- The Past Presidents of the Alumnae Association and alumnae serving as trustees to the college began meeting with the college president for an annual luncheon and update on the state of the college.

1994–95

- The Alumnae Visiting Lecture Program was begun. Outstanding alumnae were invited to the campus to spend a day speaking with classes and students.
- The Leadership Campaign was completed on June 30, 1995 exceeding the goal of $10.5 million. Grand total of commitments during the five-year campaign was over $17 million. Alumnae volunteers and their financial support played a significant role in the success of the campaign.

1996–97

- The Alumnae office began the process of securing a Columbia College license plate through the Highway department. The plate is white with a design of the columns in black and bears the letters CL, representing "Collaborative Learning" which was a prominent theme during Dr. Mitchell's presidency. These plates can be purchased through the SC Highway Department with proceeds going to the CC Alumnae Legacy Scholarship Fund.
- Dr. Peter T. Mitchell announces his resignation to become the president of Albion College, his alma mater. He was recognized by the Alumnae Association for his outstanding service to the college during Alumnae Weekend, 1997. The

luncheon was in his honor and the association presented Peter and his wife, Becky, with a grandfather clock.

- The Board of Trustees announced the 15th president of Columbia College would be Phyllis Bonanno; again alumnae volunteers hosted dinners and receptions around the state to introduce the new president.
- The alumnae strategic planning committee, appointed in 1996, met four times during the last year. This committee prepared a survey and conducted focus groups to identify the types of programs that will be beneficial to alumnae and the college in the 21st century. A detailed summary by alumnae provided information for the work of the committee. The committee presented a long range plan for the association.
- Two new initiatives, originally planned for the summer of 1998, were moved up a year, taking place in the summer of 1997. The alumnae office held a two day Volunteer Leadership Conference in the Breed Leadership Center. Sessions were conducted by the college's new president, Phyllis Bonanno, and other members of the faculty and staff. The alumnae office and the career counseling office jointly offered a Career Choices Workshop in August.

1997–99

- Phyllis O. Bonanno was appointed the college's 15th president and first woman president.
- New programs begun in the alumnae office in conjunction with the alumnae association include the following: the Alumnae Volunteer Conference; the Career Choices Seminar; Young Alumnae Homecoming in conjunction with Ludy Bowl; the Brass Apple Recognition Program—alumnae selected as Teachers of the Year are presented with an engraved brass apple; Legacy Scholarships, funded by proceeds received from the sale of the Columbia College license plates are used to provide book scholarships to the daughters and granddaughters of alumnae; the Outstanding Young Alumna Award; and the Outstanding Student Alumna Ambassador.
- In 1998, Lisa Kennerly Livingston (class of 1991) was promoted to director of Alumnae Relations. Edith Hause announced that she would retire in January 1999. The Alumnae Association honored Mrs. Hause on Alumnae Weekend 1999 by presenting her portrait to the college which hangs in the parlor of Alumnae Hall.
- Marlena Redfern Lewis (class of 1964) assumed the position of executive director of Alumnae Relations.
- The Barbara Bush Center for Science and Technology was dedicated on October

29, 1997. Major funding for the building was given by alumna, Janice Suber McNair (class of 1951).

- During this time, it was decided to model each senior class doll after the senior who was chosen by her class as Most Womanly. This was done in order to add diversity into the doll collection which would better reflect the student body and members of the Alumnae Association. Each doll in the collection represents the joining of the class into the alumnae association.
- The Alumnae Association began including a Saturday morning chapel service as part of alumnae weekend using an alumna minister or ministerial student as speaker.

1999–2000

- Marlena Lewis resigned as executive director and Lisa Kennerly Livingston (class of 1991) was appointed interim director.

2000–01

- In March, President Phyllis O. Bonanno resigned her presidency and soon after...
- Dr. James H. Rex was appointed president of Columbia College. Focus groups and receptions introducing the college's strategic plan were held all across the state and in bordering states. Edith Collins Hause (class of 1956) and Marlena Redfern Lewis Myers (class of 1964) were named special assistants to President Rex to assist in alumnae relations.
- The Alumnae Association began hosting a Friday night party for all classes during Alumnae Weekend.

2001–02

- Judy Jones Cannon (class of 1974) was appointed executive director of alumnae relations.
- The Board of Trustees revisited the plans for a five-story residence hall and revised them to build two residence cottages and a student union including a new dining facility.
- Riverbanks Zoo invited Columbia College to participate with them for the opening of the new koala exhibit.
- Harris Parker marked his 50th year at the college and was featured on the cover of *Columns*.

- Groundbreaking for the Younts Soccer Stadium built in memory of Kerry Ann Younts occurred in August as a result of a generous contribution from her parents Melvin and Dollie Isgett Younts (class of 1951).
- Dr. Caroline B. Whitson is inaugurated as the 17th president of Columbia College. Janet Alexander Cotter (class of 1956) and Virginia Crocker (class of 1973) served as co-chairs of the inauguration celebration. Alumnae hosted receptions throughout South Carolina, North Carolina and Georgia to introduce Dr. Whitson to alumnae and friends of the college.
- The Alumnae Association hosted a birthday party in honor of Dr. R. Wright Spears' 90th birthday. The celebration was held in Alumnae Hall parlor and was attended by hundreds of alumnae and friends of the college.
- The Alumnae Association was invited to join ADAPT, Alumnae Directors and Association Presidents Together, an organization of 15 women's colleges who meet annually to discuss best practices.
- The Alumnae Association began publishing a monthly electronic newsletter and held a contest for alumnae to name the publication. The winning name was *AlumnaEnews* submitted by Dr. Ellen Fagan (class of 1976).
- The Alumnae Association began hosting a graduation reception for recipients of graduate degrees and a special reception for graduates in the evening college to introduce them to the activities of the association. This event is now hosted by the Office of the Provost and the Evening College division.
- The Alumnae Association began hosting an exhibit table at the annual conference of the SC United Methodist Church. Alumnae participants at the conference are recognized with purple ribbons attached to their name tags to note alumnae involvement in the conference.
- Alumnae participated in Dr. Whitson's Committee of 100, a program to develop a strategic plan for the future of the college.

2003–04

- The Student Union opened. The Alumnae Association in conjunction with Sodexho, the corporation providing food service for the campus, provided coffee mugs for students in celebration of the new rooftop coffee shop.
- Margie L. Mitchell (class of 1983) became the Alumnae Association president, a notable moment in the association history in that she was the first woman of color to serve in this role.
- Two Charleston-style residence cottages were built on the site of the former athletic field thanks to the generosity of the Knox family and Martha Smith Kneece (class of 1955) for whom the cottages are named.

- The first Columbia College Sporting and Family Fest was held at North Camden Plantation, the home of Leonard Price, father of Kay Price Phillips (class of 1965), who helped coordinate the new fundraising event for the college.
- The Surcie Shop began opening during the day once a week for student, faculty and staff shopping.
- The association began providing "Welcome to Campus" surcies for International Students.
- The Alumnae Association began exhibiting at professional association annual conferences where alumnae would be in attendance, such as the SC Speech-Language Hearing Association, the Music Educators Conference and others in order to build professional networks for alumnae.
- The Association participated with the LA 101 course to offer a session on the history of the college and Alumnae Association for all first year students. Dr. Belinda Friedman Gergel (class of 1972), retired chair of the department of history, has been the featured speaker for this program which has become an annual event.

2004–05

- To celebrate the college's sesquicentennial anniversary, a committee of faculty, staff, alumnae and students met for a year to plan events surrounding this anniversary. Janet Alexander Cotter (class of 1956) and Ginger Crocker (class of 1973), co-chaired the committee. The chairs appointed MaryAnn Smith Eubanks Crews (class of 1959) to chair the History Committee to update the 150-year history of the college. Celebrations occurred on campus as well as in the local congregations of the United Methodist Church across South Carolina with alumnae conducting the services and hosting receptions afterwards. Every issue of *Columns* featured articles on the college's history.
- The Alumnae Association began participating with the SC UM Laity Conference at Lake Junaluska holding a luncheon with Dr. R. Wright Spears for alumnae participating in the conference and including those residing in the western North Carolina area.
- The Alumnae office and the Career Services office co-sponsored a Backpack to Briefcase seminar for graduating seniors which featured alumnae speakers offering advice on applying for jobs, interviewing and life after college.

2005–06

- Members of the classes of 1955 and 2005 held a ceremony at the time capsule outside Alumnae Hall during Alumnae Weekend 2005. The class of 1955 created the capsule, then sealed it for 100 years; the class of 2005 will be the class to open it during their 50th reunion in 2055.

2006–07

- Lisa Kennerly Livingston (class of 1991) was appointed executive director of alumnae relations.

2007–08

- Began recognizing alumnae in attendance at SCUMC annual conference with C2 name badge ribbons.
- Communication with alumnae advanced through the development of an electronic newsletter. Alumnae email addresses were collected in a variety of ways as online communication became increasingly important as a means of up to date correspondence.
- Alumnae Council assisted with the renovation of the Parlor and Tucker Conference Room using proceeds from the Surcie Shop. Major improvements were made in both rooms, including paint, wallpaper, new carpeting, flooring, and the reupholstering of some furniture.
- Formed a partnership with the Education Department and hosted a reception for graduating education majors and alumnae teachers as a mentoring opportunity.
- Alumnae outreach efforts expanded with events and meetings across Florida, Georgia, North Carolina, Tennessee, Louisiana and Mississippi.

2007–2008

- President Whitson established the "Four Cs of Leadership: Competence, Confidence, Commitment, Courage" which were associated with a student's four years on campus and incorporated into the college curriculum and alumnae messaging.
- The Four Cs became the foundation for the college's next capital campaign, the Imagine Campaign, in which the alumnae office played an integral role in planning and implementation.
- The alumnae office was engaged in the college's renewed efforts to strengthen the relationship with the South Carolina Conference of the United Methodist Church via a revised and energized church-college relations committee.

- The new college chaplain, Rev. Roy Mitchell, worked with the alumnae and development offices to coordinate church focused alumnae events to include Columbia College Sundays.
- The executive director of alumnae relations served on the conference's lay leadership team, assisting with a Laity Convocation held at Lake Junaluska each summer where an average of 300 laity attended, including many alumnae. Alumnae in attendance met for lunch with Dr. Spears.

2008–2009

- The executive director of alumnae relations provided leadership for the bishop's School of Ministry held at Springmaid Beach as yet another way of supporting the conference and engaging alumnae through a series of 16 workshops including "Spirituality and Fundraising."
- A reception was held for the first group of McNair Scholars funded by Bob and Janice Suber McNair (class of 1959).
- Lisa Livingston was named a major gifts officer while also serving as executive director of alumnae relations.
- The Men of Columbia College organization was established to involve alumnae spouses in the life of the college. Paul Yarborough, husband of Claire Wilson Yarborough (class of 1967), served as the first chairman.

2009–2010

- All special events related to the Imagine Campaign were coordinated through the alumnae office.
- A "Through These Gates" walk was held on the Saturday of Alumnae Weekend from the steps of the State House to the gates at the college.
- The Medallion and Donor Recognition Dinner was held in Edens Library to highlight the contributions for extensive enhancements and upgrades funded by Rita Eldridge Vandiver (class of 1964) and Nell Williams Overton (class of 1943) as part of the Imagine Campaign.
- The college announced the successful completion of the Imagine Campaign.
- Alumnae classes were added as a part of alumnae weekend including the first ever online social networking class called "To Friend or Not To Friend."
- Young alumnae mix and mingle events were held across the state.

2010–2011

- Communication with alumnae grew to additional electronic and social media outlets.
- Alumnae clubs meetings and other local alumnae activities continued to expand to include many new geographic locations.
- The Columbia Afternoon Club merged with the Ariail Alumnae Club.
- Sara Snell (class of 1999) was named executive director of alumnae relations.

2011–12

- CC welcomed new president, Elizabeth A. Dinndorf, J.D.
- Alumnae relations and a committee of key alumnae volunteers spearheaded the effort to introduce President Dinndorf to the CC family around the country, with events hosted by alumnae in 16 cities.
- Before assuming office, President Dinndorf attended the 2011 United Methodist Conference in Florence, meeting numerous alumnae and making vital connections within the UMC. The alumnae association hosted a luncheon for all alumnae in attendance at conference.
- After renovations to Alumnae Hall, council meetings returned "home" and began a new tradition of having lunch in Alumnae Hall.
- Alumnae Church Days continued across South Carolina. College chaplain Reverend Roy Mitchell, President Dinndorf, and often the Hi-Cs visited many UMCs, bringing greetings and updates from the college.
- The alumnae weekend Friday night party moved to campus as a reception for all classes, to officially kick off the weekend's events.
- The alumnae council continued the tradition of welcoming legacy freshman with visits to Asbury Hall on move-in day.
- The annual faculty-staff Christmas coffee was moved to Tuesday morning during exam week, so that President Dinndorf could attend.
- The president of the alumnae association became a non-voting member of the Board of Trustees.

2012–13

- Student alumnae ambassadors, the student arm of the alumnae association, was revived on campus and welcomed a group of many students in its first year. The students helped with council meetings, alumnae weekend and all alumnae activities on and off campus.
- Alumnae weekend format changed to include the addition of afternoon

sessions offered to all attendees. Garden workshops, book discussions and other topics were offered and well-attended.

- The alumnae association began hosting a reception before the CC Choir's presentation of the service of lessons and carols. The sidewalk from Alumnae Hall to College Place UMC was lined with luminaries, bought by alumnae in honor or memory of loved ones.
- A new Lake Junaluska alumnae luncheon began as an early celebration of Dr. Spears' birthday, and became an annual luncheon event for alumnae in and around the Lake Junaluska area.

2013–14

- CC was the host for the 2013 ADAPT Conference (Alumnae Directors and Presidents Together). Held in November, 24 alumnae directors and alumnae presidents from women's colleges attended the three-day conference.
- AlumnaEnews switched to a new format, with more graphics allowing readers to click on specific articles to access the text. This began the use of AlumnaEnews as a vehicle to track lost alumnae, share "sneak peeks" of class news, and celebrate accomplishments of CC athletics.
- The online Surcie Shop was launched, offering apparel, home décor and accessories with the college logo; products were different from those offered in the bookstore and could be shipped anywhere.
- Mitzi's Garden was dedicated during alumnae weekend; additionally, two honorary alumnae were named: Barbara Knox Cobb and Kathy Coleman Knox.
- Mitzi's Garden was lit with luminaries for guests to enjoy on their way to the service of lessons and carols.
- Ludy Bowl 101, a memorabilia exhibit, was presented in Alumnae Hall during Ludy Bowl weekend. This visual history of Miss Ludy and past Ludy Bowl games was on display for all campus visitors.
- The alumnae association partnered with the chaplain's office and the CC Choir during the spring tour to Lake Junaluska. Area alumnae were invited to the choir performance and encouraged to attend the local church service the following day for the CC service.
- The alumnae association funded the purchase of plantation shutters for Tucker Conference Room in Alumnae Hall. The association also funded the refurbishment of both sofas in the parlor.
- Alumnae were actively involved in selecting recipients for the Momentum Scholarship, and were invited to nominate outstanding high school juniors to apply for the scholarship. Alumnae also played a key role in the interview

process to award the scholarships.

- The alumnae association became an active partner of the mentor program through the leadership institute. Alumnae were matched with first-year students for year-long mentoring relationships.

2014–15

- In addition to visiting and welcoming legacy students in McNair Hall on move-in day, the alumnae association also sponsored a water station and hospitality tent on the mall during the afternoon of move-in day, which served as a welcome break for parents and new first years.
- Ludy Bowl 101 continued to delight campus visitors during Ludy Bowl weekend.
- Live Purple, the young alumnae arm of the alumnae association, began to host monthly get-togethers at restaurants around Columbia.
- Carla Lewis Moore (class of 1994) resigned her position as president of the alumnae association in order to serve as interim director of alumnae relations.

2015–16

- Carla Lewis Moore (class of 1994) was named executive director of alumnae relations. All programs continued and alumnae participation for on and off-campus activities was re-energized.
- The alumnae association mourned the death of beloved President Emeritus R. Wright Spears. A reception was held in Alumnae Hall after the memorial service at College Place UMC.
- The Sisters Garden, a beautification project located near the columns, was dedicated during alumnae weekend.
- The college and alumnae relations office participated in events throughout the year, both on campus and in the community, to commemorate the centennial of Georgia O'Keeffe's teaching art at the college.
- Social media efforts increased including the creation of class Facebook pages.

2016–2017

- Funds from the proceeds of the Surcie Shop were used to replace the flooring in Tucker Conference Room.
- Updates to the parlor were made to include painting, new flooring, the addition of new chandeliers, cleaning of the lambrequins and upholstery refurbishings.
- The doll collection was carefully cleaned, photographed and catalogued.

- Alumnae Hall was renamed Janet Alexander Cotter Alumnae Hall with a dedication ceremony and reception held during alumnae weekend.
- The first alumnae Easter egg hunt was held near the columns with great success.
- The student alumnae association continued to grow and provided valuable support for alumnae association activities.
- Tony Pickett, long-time college employee and friend to all alums, was honored by a group of alumnae for his dedication to the college and support of alumnae events.

Compiled by Edith Collins Hause (class of 1956), Judy Jones Cannon (class of 1974) and Lisa Kennerly Livingston (class of 1991).

The first portion of this article is a synopsis of an outstanding history of the Alumnae Association from 1882 through 1979 written by Alawee Gibson Tucker (class of 1939) and Sara Brabham Eastman (class of 1945). It is a part of chapter six of the book *Columbia College, The Ariail Era*, edited by the late Dr. Jerold Savory, a member of the English department faculty and college administrator. The continuation of the history of the Alumnae Association in this book is a chronological documentation of programs and traditions that have been planned and implemented by the Alumnae Council, the governing body of the Association, and the Alumnae Office and supported by the Alumnae Association.

Resources for historical information include Chapter 6, "What In Life Our Lot Shall Be" by Alawee Gibson Tucker (class of 1939) and Sara Brabham Eastman (class of 1945) from *Columbia College: The Ariail Era* by Jerold Savory and *Columbia College 1912–1968* by J.M. Ariail.

APPENDIX B: AWARD RECIPIENTS

ALUMNAE ASSOCIATION DISTINGUISHED SERVICE AWARD

1978	Wil Lou Gray (class of 1903)
1979	Belva Haynsworth Ariail (class of 1925)
1980	Alawee Gibson Tucker (class of 1939)
1981	Niven McGill Cantwell (class of 1918) and Ruth Crary Miller (class of 1918)
1982	Sara Brabham Eastman (class of 1942)
1983	Clelia Derrick Hendrix (class of 1941)
1984	Janet Alexander Cotter (class of 1956)
1985	Anne Turner Harrell (class of 1957)
1986	Barbara Buchan Shealy (class of 1933)
1987	MaryAnn Smith Eubanks Crews (class of 1959)
1988	Jennie Cottingham Henry (class of 1928)
1989	Becky Baker Pugh (class of 1962)
1990	Anne Beebe (class of 1950)
1991	Marjorie Faucett Patterson (class of 1949)
1992	Mabel Shull Gantt (class of 1938)
1993	Carol Fanning Brown (class of 1939)
1994	Jewel Hardee Shaw (class of 1940), Lula Hardee Hill (class of 1935), and Mitchell Hardee Taylor (class of 1936)
1995	Louise Springs Crews (class of 1942)
1996	Sarah Blakely Skenes (class of 1955)
1997	Helen Duensing Sanders (class of 1936)
1998	Meg Ward Pace (class of 1962)
1999	Eva Davis York (class of 1934)
2000	Elizabeth DuRant (class of 1950)
2001	Virginia Thompson Paysinger (class of 1939)
2002	Ann Buckwalter Salter (class of 1955)

2003	Edith Collins Hause (class of 1956)
2004	Marlena Redfern Myers (class of 1964)
2005	Betty Ulmer McGregor (class of 1951)
2006	Cornelia Rickenbacker Freeman (class of 1933)
2007	Kathryn Verdery Cannon (class of 1955)
2008	Barbara Courtney Thomas (class of 1957)
2009	Nell Williams Overton (class of 1943)
2010	Martha Smith Kneece (class of 1955)
2011	Jewell Powell Hill (class of 1960)
2012	Mary Ann Reeves Phillips (class of 1956)
2013	Elizabeth Johnson Patterson (class of 1961)
2014	Katherine Jeannette Price (class of 1993)
2015	Judy Jones Cannon (class of 1974)
2016	Marsha Steele Moore (class of 1970)

WIL LOU GRAY OUTSTANDING EDUCATOR AWARD

1985	Frankie Ellis Newman (class of 1949)
1986	Aileen Gramling McGill (class of 1918)
1987	Eddie Graham (class of 1960)
1988	Idella Fallow Bodie (class of 1946)
1989	Ruth Stockman Pugh (class of 1924)
1990	Margaret McLeod Edwards (class of 1941)
1991	Dr. Frances Clayton Welch (class of 1969)
1992	Hazel Floyd Goodale (class of 1951)
1993	Charlene Northcutt Herring (class of 1971)
1994	Anne Reynolds Stewart (class of 1951)
1995	Thema Rast (class of 1945)
1996	Arie Black Guess (class of 1949)
1997	Dr. Rebecca Glover Swanson (class of 1957)
1998	Thomasine Dabbs Muzekari (class of 1983)
1999	Sandra Byrd (class of 1983) and Mary Holler Rice (class of 1929)
2000	Carolyn Tuten Ross (class of 1966)
2001	Louise Speake Wood (class of 1964)
2002	Dr. Roberta Linder Ferrell (class of 1964)
2003	Dr. Mary Tuck Kennerly (class of 1968)
2004	Paula Brafford Wilson (class of 1974)
2005	Dayle Marchette Timmons (class of 1971)
2006	Nancy Jackson Gregory (class of 1976)
2007	Elizabeth Wilson Patenaude (class of 1974)
2008	Julieanne LeJeune Humowitz (class of 1992)

2009	Elizabeth Boozer Dalton (class of 1956)
2010	Deborah Sliver Stroman (class of 1984)
2011	Mitzi Winesett (class of 1970)
2012	Sara L. Nalley (class of 1963)
2013	Jenny Crowder Johansson (class of 2001)
2014	Anna Elizabeth Miller (class of 1995)
2015	Dr. Margaret Stafford Parker (class of 1970)
2016	Elizabeth Ann Phibbs (class of 1977)

Outstanding Young Alumna Award

1999	Margaret Price Creech (class of 1990)
2000	Rebecca Williams Smith (class of 1991)
2001	Melissa Tuten Stone (class of 1994)
2002	Acacia Bamberg Salatti (class of 1994)
2003	Dawn Manous Steeves (class of 1999)
2004	Caroline Earp (class of 2000)
2005	Sara Snell (class of 1999)
2006	Jamila Harrington Hudley (class of 1997)
2007	Marley Lybrand Douglas (class of 2004)
2008	Ruth Anne Reeves O'Cain (class of 1994)
2009	Ciona Deneé Rouse (class of 2001)
2010	Nan Binnarr Carter (class of 2004)
2011	Tiffany Denise Knowlin (class of 2003)
2013	Chelsea Elizabeth Eichorn (class of 2008)
2014/2015	Ginny Skinner Haynes (class of 2001)
2016	Omotola Seun-Adeyemi (class of 2012)

Career Achievement Award

1985	Jo Graham Foster (class of 1935) and Charlotte Stevenson (class of 1923)
1986	Joan Vaughan Young (class of 1956)
1987	Hazel Melia (class of 1938)
1988	Elizabeth Johnston Patterson (class of 1961)
1989	Ann Hatton Lewis (class of 1922)
1990	Emmalee Gaddy Robbins (class of 1963)
1991	Kathryn Wise Baxley (class of 1947)
1992	Linda Jones DuRant (class of 1968)
1993	Claire Wilson Yarborough (class of 1967)
1994	Karen Johnson Williams (class of 1972)
1995	Gussie Kennerly Johnson (class of 1935)

1996	Caroline Watson (class of 1982)
1997	Rebecca Laffitte (class of 1977)
1998	Ann Pringle Washington (class of 1991)
1999	Dr. Elizabeth Gressette (class of 1970)
2000	Mary Margaret Harper Wilkins (class of 1980)
2001	Carole Dunaway Howell (class of 1975)
2002	Denise Turbeville Barker (class of 1976)
2003	Lisa Wheeler Rossi (class of 1987)
2004	Anne Gasque Depta (class of 1958)
2005	Dr. Elaine Kirby Ferraro (class of 1972)
2006	Tamera Norton Smith (class of 1990)
2007	Katherine R. Ligon (class of 1974)
2008	LaTisha Gotell Faulks (class of 1996)
2009	Deidre Buice Crow (class of 1972)
2010	Moo Gordon Brockington (class of 1981)
2011	Jane London McIntyre (class of 1968)
2012	Patsy Rauton Lightle (class of 1976)
2013	Bootsie Harvie Wynne (class of 1983)
2014	Stacey Deane Maxwell (class of 1991)
2015	Regina Dawn Lemmon (class of 1997)
2016	Kathleen Aughtry Randall (class of 1973)

ALUMNAE ASSOCIATION PRESIDENT'S AWARD

2003	Peggy Makins (class of 1994)
2004	Ruth Suddath Green (class of 1945), Nathalie Gregg (class of 1986), and Doris Durante Kahn (honorary alumna)
2005	Kimberly Rose (class of 1994) and Marie Locker Hill (honorary alumna)
2011	Lisa K. Livingston (class of 1991)

Appendix C: Alumnae Association Leaders

Alumnae Directors

1926–1928	Emmie Wright (class of 1912)
1937–1939	Sarah Bolt Owens (class of 1918)
1940–1941	Merrill Bennet Nichols (class of 1919)
1941–1942	Christine Smith (class of 1938)
1948–1949	Belva Haynsworth Ariail (class of 1925)
1949–1951	Marjorie Faucett Patterson (class of 1949)
1953–1957	Ruth Henry Lightsey (class of 1928)
1957–1959	Janet Alexander Cotter (class of 1956)
1959–1964	Nancy Williams Johnson (class of 1955)
1964–1970	MaryAnn Smith Eubanks Crews (class of 1959)
1970–1972	Carol Lee Milhous (class of 1963)
1972–1974	Gail Rigby Kennedy Phillips (class of 1969)
1974–1984	Edith Collins Hause (class of 1956)
1985–1990	Charlotte Stackhouse Broome (class of 1975)
1991–1999	Edith Collins Hause (class of 1956)
1999–2000	Marlena Redfern Lewis Myers (class of 1964)
2000–2006	Judy Jones Cannon (class of 1974)
2006–2011	Lisa Kennerly Livingston (class of 1991)
2011–2014	Sara Snell Johnson (class of 1999)
2014–	Carla Lewis Moore (class of 1994)

Alumnae Association Presidents

1882–1888	Jane Herbert Haynes (class of 1876)
1888–1896	Ellen Stanley Watkins (class of 1884)

1896–1898	Helen McMaster (class of 1875)
1898–1899	Anna Smith Rice (class of 1884)
1899–1900	Ellen Jenny
1900–1903	Harriet Glaze Burrows (class of 1860)
1903–1908	Blanche Jones (class of 1880)
1908–1909	Marie McDonald (class of 1901)
1909–1910	Julia Phillips Stanley (class of 1894)
1910–1914	Alma Daniel Watson (class of 1906)
1914–1915	Willie Daniel Sidberry (class of 1907)
1915–1917	Omega Ellerbe (class of 1883)
1917–1918	Rowena Aull Daniel (class of 1882)
1918–1920	Olive Counts (class of 1912)
1920–1923	Marie Zimmerman Burnett (class of 1910)
1923–1924	Kate Glenn Hardin (class of 1905)
1924–1926	Wil Lou Gray (class of 1903)
1926–1928	Elise Tiller Spigner (class of 1904)
1928–1929	Corrie Haselden Edwards (class of 1893)
1929–1933	Belva Haynsworth Ariail (class of 1925)
1933–1935	Permelia Jennings Strohecker (class of 1919)
1935–1937	Lessie Tiller Fleming (class of 1908)
1937–1939	Margaret Milhous Richardson (class of 1921)
1939–1941	Louise Bennett Neeley (class of 1922)
1941–1942	Reba Caroll Taylor (class of 1922)
1942–1943	Lula Delle Snyder Brown (class of 1939)
1943–1944	Ella May Atkinson (class of 1911)
1944–1946	Mozelle McCarley Malone (class of 1922)
1946–1950	Belva Haynsworth Ariail (class of 1925)
1950–1952	Vernell Buie Miley (class of 1922)
1952–1954	Myrtle Higginbatham Groeschel
1954–1956	Permelia Jennings Strohecker (class of 1919)
1956–1959	Eva Crosby Covington (class of 1925)
1959–1961	Mary Hill Johnson
1961–1963	Mary Chandler Roper (class of 1930)
1963–1965	Alawee Gibson Tucker (class of 1939)
1965–1967	Sara Brabham Eastman (class of 1942)
1967–1969	Katherine Bauknight Betsill (class of 1950)
1969–1971	Marian Touchberry Taylor (class of 1945)
1971–1973	Janet Alexander Cotter (class of 1956)
1973–1975	Mae Blackwell Thomson (class of 1959)
1975–1977	Patsy Cave Whitaker (class of 1955)
1977–1979	Ann Buckwalter Salter (class of 1955)

1979–1981	Anne Turner Harrell (class of 1957)
1981–1983	Becky Baker Pugh (class of 1962)
1983–1985	MaryAnn Smith Eubanks Crews (class of 1959)
1985–1987	Anne Beebe (class of 1950)
1987–1989	Kathryn Verdery Cannon (class of 1955)
1989–1991	Betty Ulmer McGregor (class of 1951)
1991–1993	Linda Sue Neal Smith (class of 1964)
1993–1995	Judy Jones Cannon (class of 1974)
1995–1997	Carol Stackhouse (class of 1974)
1997–1999	Nancy Burch Bunch (class of 1972)
1999–2001	Emil Burns Mitchell (class of 1984)
2001–2003	Bootsie Harvie Wynne (class of 1983)
2003–2005	Margie L. Mitchell (class of 1983)
2005–2007	Carole Dunaway Howell (class of 1975)
2007–2009	Candy Crane Shuler (class of 1973)
2009–2011	Rebecca Glover Swanson (class of 1957)
2011–2013	Marlena Redfern Myers (class of 1964)
2013–2015	Carla Lewis Moore (class of 1994)
2015–2017	Charlotte Stackhouse Broome (class of 1975)

COLUMBIA COLLEGE MEDALLION RECIPIENTS

1980	Lucille "Ludy" Ellerbe Godbold; Belva Haynsworth Ariail (class of 1925); Clelia Derrick Hendrix (class of 1941); William J. Colvin, Jr.; T.J. Harrelson, Jr.
1981	Bernard S. Drennan; Alawee Gibson Tucker (class of 1939); Anne Frierson Griffin (class of 1924); Fred Howard Parker
1982	J. Drake Edens, Jr.; Grace Killingsworth Turner (class of 1915); Eben Taylor; Leon S. Goodall, Jr.; Arthur L. Humphries
1983	Wil Lou Gray (class of 1903); Ruth Henry Lightsey (class of 1928); Thomas G. Shuler; Marshall A. Shearouse; Janet Alexander Cotter (class of 1956)
1984	Niven McGill Cantwell (class of 1918); A. McKay Brabham, Jr.; Cornelia Rickenbacker Freeman (class of 1933); R. Wright Spears
1985	Zach Daniel; Jennie Cottingham Henry (class of 1928); Sara Brabham Eastman (class of 1942); Mary Lou Kramer; J.E. Reeves, Jr.
1986	Mary Chandler Roper (class of 1930); Thomas P. Knox, Jr.; Blance Allen Mirse; MaryAnn Smith Eubanks Crews (class of 1959); Leon Joe Penner, Jr.
1987	Margarette Richards; R.H. Smith; Marion A. Knox, Sr.; Elizabeth Wilson; Josephine B. Abney
1988	Mary Blue Spears; William C. Stackhouse; Virginia Thompson Paysinger

(class of 1939); Mabel Shull Gantt (class of 1938); William H. Orders

1989	W. Jackson Greer; Ruth Crary Miller (class of 1918); Marcus R. Durlach, Jr.; Robert J. Maxwell, Jr.; Eva Davis York (class of 1934)
1990	Sybil Shaffer Blackston (class of 1928); Sara L. Mott; Shelby Davis Sansbury (class of 1964); Charles G. Pfeiffer
1991	Aracelis G. Shaw; Madeline Yongue Allen; Charles A. Bundy; Marjorie Faucett Patterson (class of 1949); Susie Thomas
1992	Anne Beebe (class of 1950); Carl Milton Tucker, Jr.; William Charles Reid; David Joseph Haigler; Mary Adams Brown
1993	Janie Farmer Myers (class of 1937); Sarah M. Dawsey; Annie Laurie Kennerly George (class of 1933); Gibert Guthrie Darr; Harold Boyd Risher
1994	Rachel Spivey Knox; David E. Baker; Mae Blackwell Thomson (class of 1959); Robert Timothy Barham; Janice Suber McNair (class of 1959)
1995	Sibyl Causey Leggett (class of 1950); Thomas Whitfield Dunaway, Jr.; Guy F. Lipscomb, Jr.; Ann Buckwalter Salter (class of 1955); George Cochran Fant, Jr.
1996	Samuel T. Middleton; William E. Sellars, Sr.; Jane Castles Brooks (class of 1958); Elizabeth DuRant (class of 1950); Patricia Cave Whitaker (class of 1955)
1997	Jerold James Savory; Ralph Thomas Mirse; Helen Addison Wingard (class of 1935); Seldon Kennedy Smith; Clarie Wilson Yarborough (class of 1968)
1998	William Warren Butler; John Thomas Mundy; Harris Hartwell Parker, Jr.; Cynthia Byrd Gilliam; Mary Ann Reeves Phillips (class of 1956)
1999	Roy & Marnie Pearce; Miriam Freeman Rawl; Scott Shanklin Peterson (class of 1966)
2000	Hannah Campbell Meadors (class of 1956); Nell WIlliams Overton (class of 1943); Jack S. Hupp; J. Rhett Jackson, Jr.
2001	Sindey J. Palmer; Louise Springs Crews (class of 1942); Rebecca Glover Swanson (class of 1957); Virginia Uldrick
2002	Jennifer Brewer Mungo; Edmund Perry Palmer; Betty Livingston Bruner; Anne Turner Harrell (class of 1957); Martha Smith Kneece (class of 1955)
2003	Paula Harper Bethea; Virginia L. Crocker (class of 1973); Edith Collins Hause (class of 1956); J. Joseph Mitchell, Jr.; Peter T. Mitchell
2004	R. Wright Spears
2005	Helen Nelson Grant (class of 1981); Robert J. Moore; Elizabeth Johnston Patterson (class of 1961); M. Edward Sellers
2006	Johnnie Cordell Breed; Belinda Friedman Gergel (class of 1972); Dorothy M. Pickett
2007	Gene & Catherine Eaker; Marshall L. Meadors, Jr.

2008	Linda H. Short; Karen Johnson Williams (class of 1972)
2009	Vivia Lawton Fowler (class of 1976); Jan Love; Betty Ulmer McGregor (class of 1951)
2010	Marlena Redfern Myers (class of 1964); Candy Y. Waites
2011	Leonard L. Price; Ellen Claussen Davis (class of 1972)
2013	Rita Eldridge Vandiver (class of 1964); Larry Wilson
2014	Joseph Rozier Blanchard; Marion A. Knox, Jr.; Lynn Stokes Murray (class of 1983); Joanna Batson Stone (class of 1947)
2015	Jim B. Apple; Terry Collier; Jane London McIntyre (class of 1968)

ALUMNAE MEMBERS OF THE BOARD OF TRUSTEES

Wil Lou Gray (class of 1903)[44]
Ivah Epps Frierson (class of 1897)[45]
Elizabeth Gamble Epps (class of 1923)
Jennie Cottingham Henry (class of 1928)
Grace Killingsworth Turner (class of 1915)
Clelia Derrick Hendrix (class of 1941)[46]
Alawee Gibson Tucker (class of 1939)
Sara Brabham Eastman (class of 1942)
Anne Beebe (class of 1950)
Lillie Edens Herndon (class of 1986)
Liz Johnston Patterson (class of 1961)
Janet Alexander Cotter (class of 1956)
Kathryn Verdery Cannon (class of 1955)
Ellen Claussen Davis (class of 1972)
Jill Hauenstein (class of 1970)
Martha Smith Kneece (class of 1955)
Jane Castles Brooks (class of 1958)
Florence Browning Appleby (class of 1950)
MaryAnn Smith Eubanks Crews (class of 1959)
Diane Smith McKay (class of 1974)
Shelby Davis Sansbury (class of 1964)
Helen Nelson Grant (class of 1981)
Diane Moseley (class of 1967)
June Johnson Bradham (class of 1968)
Annette Williams Lynn (class of 1975)
Nancy Cummings Humphries (class of 1972)

---

44 Appointed by the conference to the Board of Trustees in 1925
45 Appointed by the conference to the Board of Trustees in 1925
46 First woman chair of Board of Trustees

Cynthia Pryor Hardy (class of 1998)
Jean Ellen Duke (class of 1977)
Rita Eldridge Vandiver (class of 1964)
Kay Price Phillips (class of 1965)
Carol Rich Storey (class of 1968)
Danielle Saunders Walsh (class of 1991)
Claire Wilson Yarborough (class of 1968)
Rebecca Laffitte (class of 1977)
Mary M. Cantando (class of 1985)
Pat Stone Wood (class of 1964)
Ruth Ann McCarter Collins (class of 1968)
Marsha Steele Moore (class of 1970)
Marlena Redfern Lewis Myers (class of 1964)[47]
Carla Lewis Moore (class of 1994)[48]
Charlotte Stackhouse Broome (class of 1975)[49]

Beginning with Marlena Redfern Lewis, the Board of Directors approved having the President of the Alumnae Association attend board meetings. Carla Lewis Moore and Charlotte Stackhouse Broome attended as president of the Alumnae Association during their terms of office.

---

47 Began as President of AA, then elected to serve.
48 Attended meetings as President of the Alumnae Association
49 Attended meetings as President of the Alumnae Association.

SUPPORT FOR THIS VOLUME

The book *We Thy Glory Sing: Snapshots & Remembrances from the History of Columbia College, 1854–2016* would not have been possible but for the hard work of the Sesquicentennial Committee and the History Sub-Committee, as well as the generosity of those who contributed financially to its production. Much gratitude is extended to those donors, whom we are pleased to recognize with our heartfelt thanks.

Dr. & Mrs. M. Donald Alexander, Jr.
Alumnae Club Aiken County
Mrs. Patricia Meek Boggs
Mrs. Elaine Taylor Brantley
Mrs. Charlotte Stackhouse Broome
Mrs. Judy Jones Cannon
Mrs. Kathryn Verdery Cannon
Central Carolina Community Foundation
Charlestone Area Columbia College Alumnae Club
Mrs. Barbara Knox Cobb
Columbia College Evening Club
Mrs. L. Arlen Cotter
Mrs. MaryAnn Smith Eubanks Crews
Ms. Elizabeth DuRant
Mrs. Linda Jones DuRant
Mrs. Carolyn B. Emeneker
Mrs. Mary Daley Evans
Dr. Elaine Kirby Ferraro
Mrs. Annie Laurie Kennerly George
Dr. Belinda Friedman Gergel
Mr. & Mrs. William Charles Gillespie
Mrs. Carol Stackhouse Hall
Mrs. Belva Smith Hamer
Mrs. Anne Turner Harrell
Mrs. Edith Collins Hause
Mrs. Mary Finley Henderson (D)
Marie Locker Hill-Chapiesky (D)

Mrs. Jamila Harrington Hudley
Mrs. Nancy Cummings Humphries
Mr. Jack S. Hupp
Mrs. Marion A. Knox, Jr.
Ms. Rebecca Laffitte
Mrs. Marlene Deloach Lamar (D)
Ms. Lisa Kennerly Livingston
Mrs. Betty Ulmer McGregor
Mrs. Dianna Smith McKay
Mrs. Emil Burns Mitchell
Mr. J. Joseph Mitchell
Dr. Peter T. Mitchell
Mrs. Mary Epps Monroe
Mrs. Carla Lewis Moore
Mrs. Elizabeth Alexander Murdaugh
Mrs. Marlena Redfern Myers
Mrs. Liz Johnston Patterson
Mrs. Marjorie Faucett Patterson
Mrs. Mary Ann Reeves Phillips
Mrs. Shelby Davis Sansbury
Mr. Jeffrey H. Selig
Rev. Rebecca Joyner Shirley
Rev. R. Wright Spears (D)
The Redmond Corporation
Dr. Alawee Gibson Tucker (D)
Mrs. Rita Eldridge Vandiver
Mr. Larry Wilson
Mrs. Joan Vaughan Young

www.ingramcontent.com/pod-product-compliance
Lightning Source LLC
Chambersburg PA
CBHW040857100426
42813CB00015B/2827